St. Francis of Assisi

G. K. CHESTERTON

St. Francis of Assisi

Foreword by Joseph F. Girzone,
author of *Joshua*

IMAGE BOOKS
DOUBLEDAY
New York London Toronto Sydney Auckland

An Image Book
PUBLISHED BY DOUBLEDAY
a division of Bantam Doubleday Dell Publishing Group, Inc.
1540 Broadway, New York, New York 10036

IMAGE, DOUBLEDAY, and the portrayal of a deer drinking from
a stream are trademarks of Doubleday, a division of Bantam
Doubleday Dell Publishing Group, Inc.

First Image edition published February 1957
by special arrangement with Doubleday.
This Image edition published 1990.

ISBN 0-385-02900-4

Library of Congress Catalog Number 57-1230

Foreword

Watching a child at play is fun. Children live in their own little world and to them it is serious business, and in their minds it all makes sense. We smile at them. They can accept our smiling. To laugh at them is hurtful and damaging and causes them to run from us and hide. As adults we have long lost the key to the beauty of that child world. We can look at it from a distance, see the joy and adventure that flows with such spontaneity from a child's imagination, but we can no longer enter into that world. It is lost to us forever. We were once there but somewhere along life's path have lost the key to the door that unlocks that world for us.

We might be tempted to call the child's world a world of make-believe. But that would be a mistake. It is make-believe to us who have found another world which we never dare to call make-believe. That child's world is no more fantasy to the child than our unhealthy world is to ourselves.

When we look upon the lives of the saints we run headlong into the same phenomenon. Their lives appear to be almost fiction, make-believe, and not reality. We call them dreamers. We call them psychotic. We call them a variety of names because we cannot grasp the significance or the relevance of their

5

actions to our world of make-believe. We make statues of St. Francis and recite his prayer of peace. Our frightened world desperately grabs hold of his memory in a frantic attempt to protect our environment from pollution, but we don't really take him seriously. We have merely adopted him as a pet or mascot, without ever really grasping the real meaning of his life.

Indeed, to read his life in the accounts of most biographers is like reading a catalogue of episodes almost as weird as those related in *Raiders of the Lost Ark* or a James Bond movie. The story of Francis is quaint, but not to be taken seriously, and if, God forbid, any of our children started to do some of the things Francis did we would no doubt bring the child screaming, not to a bishop, as Francis's father did, but to a psychiatrist, which was unheard of in those days.

The remarkable genius of G. K. Chesterton, in this little life of St. Francis, is that he has found the key to entering the apparently make-believe world of the saint and has made it possible for the reader to understand the underlying logic of how God could respond to a human who took Him seriously, and could touch his life with a magic from still another real world.

In this little story, St. Francis isn't a dreamer. He was the world as it really was in his day, a world that professed belief in God, but mocked Him by its everyday drama. Francis found God, and happened to fall in love with Him, so he could see the world as God saw it and spent his life mocking the world in all its absurdity, and enjoyed completely his role as God's "Jongleur," trying to bring back God's children to a real understanding of what it means to be the children of God.

—JOSEPH F. GIRZONE

CONTENTS

CHAPTER I

The Problem of St. Francis

A sketch of St. Francis of Assisi in modern English may be written in one of three ways. Between these the writer must make his selection; and the third way, which is adopted here, is in some respects the most difficult of all. At least, it would be the most difficult if the other two were not impossible.

First, he may deal with this great and most amazing man as a figure in secular history and a model of social virtues. He may describe this divine demagogue as being, as he probably was, the world's one quite sincere democrat. He may say (what means very little) that St. Francis was in advance of his age. He may say (what is quite true) that St. Francis anticipated all that is most liberal and sympathetic in the modern mood; the love of nature; the love of animals; the sense of social compassion; the sense of the spiritual dangers of prosperity and even of property. All those things that nobody understood before Wordsworth were familiar to St. Francis. All those things that were first discovered by Tolstoy had been taken for granted by St. Francis.

He could be presented, not only as a human but a humanitarian hero; indeed as the first hero of humanism. He has been described as a sort of morning star of the Renaissance. And in comparison with all these things, his ascetical theology can be ignored or dismissed as a contemporary accident, which was fortunately not a fatal accident. His religion can be regarded as a superstition, but an inevitable superstition, from which not even genius could wholly free itself; in the consideration of which it would be unjust to condemn St. Francis for his self-denial or unduly chide him for his chastity. It is quite true that even from so detached a standpoint his stature would still appear heroic. There would still be a great deal to be said about the man who tried to end the Crusades by talking to the Saracens or who interceded with the Emperor for the birds. The writer might describe in a purely historical spirit the whole of that great Franciscan inspiration that was felt in the painting of Giotto, in the poetry of Dante, in the miracle plays that made possible the modern drama, and in so many other things that are already appreciated by the modern culture. He may try to do it, as others have done, almost without raising any religious question at all. In short, he may try to tell the story of a saint without God; which is like being told to write the life of Nansen and forbidden to mention the North Pole.

Second, he may go to the opposite extreme, and decide, as it were, to be defiantly devotional. He may make the theological enthusiasm as thoroughly the theme as it was the theme of the first Franciscans. He may treat religion as the real thing that it was to the real Francis of Assisi. He can find an austere joy, so to speak, in parading the paradoxes of asceticism and all the holy topsy-turvydom of humility. He can stamp the whole history with the Stigmata, record fasts like fights against a dragon; till in the vague modern mind St. Francis is as dark a figure as St. Dominic. In short he can produce what many in our world will regard as a sort of photographic negative, the reversal of all lights and shades; what the foolish will find as impenetrable as darkness and even many of the wise will find almost as invisible as if it were written in silver upon white. Such a study of St. Francis would be unintelligible to any one who does not share his religion, perhaps only partly intelligible to any one who does not share his vocation. According to degrees of judgment, it will be regarded as something too bad or too good for the world. The only difficulty about doing the thing in this way is that it cannot be done. It would really require a saint to write the life of a saint. In the present case the objections to such a course are insuperable.

Third, he may try to do what I have tried to do here; and, as I have already suggested, the course has peculiar problems of its own. The writer may put himself in the position of the ordinary modern outsider and enquirer; as indeed the present writer is still largely and was once entirely in that position. He may start from the standpoint of a man who already admires St. Francis, but only for those things which such a man finds admirable. In other words he may assume that the reader is at least as enlightened as Renan or Matthew Arnold; but in the light of that enlightenment he may try to illuminate what Renan and Matthew Arnold left dark. He may try to use what is understood to explain what is not understood. He may say to the modern English reader: "Here is an historical character which is admittedly attractive to many of us already, by its gaiety, its romantic imagination, its spiritual courtesy and camaraderie, but which also contains elements (evidently equally sincere and emphatic) which seem to you quite remote and repulsive. But after all, this man was a man and not half a dozen men. What seems inconsistency to you did not seem inconsistency to him. Let us see whether we can understand, with the help of the existing understanding, these other things that seem now to be doubly dark, by their intrinsic gloom and their ironic contrast." I do not mean, of course, that I can really reach such a psychological completeness in this crude and curt outline. But I mean that this is the only controversial condition that I shall here assume; that I am dealing with the sympathetic outsider. I shall not assume any more or any less agreement than this. A materialist may not care whether the inconsistencies are reconciled or not. A Catholic may not see any inconsistencies to reconcile. But I am here addressing the ordinary modern man, sympathetic but sceptical, and I can only rather hazily hope that, by approaching the great saint's story through what is evidently picturesque and popular about it, I may at least leave the reader understanding a little more than he did before of the consistency of a complete character; that by approaching it in this way, we may at least get a glimmering of why the poet who praised his lord the sun, often hid himself in a dark cavern, of why the saint who was so gentle with his Brother the Wolf was so harsh to his Brother the Ass

(as he nicknamed his own body), of why the troubadour who said that love set his heart on fire sepa-
rated himself from women, of why the singer who
rejoiced in the strength and gaiety of the fire deliberately rolled himself in the snow, of why the very
song which cries with all the passion of a pagan,
"Praised be God for our Sister, Mother Earth, which
brings forth varied fruits and grass and glowing
flowers," ends almost with the words "Praised be
God for our Sister, the death of the body."

Renan and Matthew Arnold failed utterly at this
test. They were content to follow Francis with their
praises until they were stopped by their prejudices;
the stubborn prejudices of the sceptic. The moment
Francis began to do something they did not understand or did not like, they did not try to understand
it, still less to like it; they simply turned their backs
on the whole business and "walked no more with
him." No man will get any further along a path of
historical enquiry in that fashion. These sceptics are
really driven to drop the whole subject in despair,
to leave the most simple and sincere of all historical
characters as a mass of contradictions, to be praised
on the principle of the curate's egg. Arnold refers to
the asceticism of Alverno almost hurriedly, as if it
were an unlucky but undeniable blot on the beauty
of the story; or rather as if it were a pitiable break-
down and bathos at the end of the story. Now this
is simply to be stone-blind to the whole point of any
story. To represent Mount Alverno as the mere collapse of Francis is exactly like representing Mount
Calvary as the mere collapse of Christ. Those mountains are mountains, whatever else they are, and it
is nonsense to say (like the Red Queen) that they

are comparative hollows or negative holes in the ground. They were quite manifestly meant to be culminations and landmarks. To treat the Stigmata as a sort of scandal, to be touched on tenderly but with pain, is exactly like treating the original five wounds of Jesus Christ as five blots on His character. You may dislike the idea of asceticism; you may dislike equally the idea of martyrdom; for that matter you may have an honest and natural dislike of the whole conception of sacrifice symbolised by the cross. But if it is an intelligent dislike, you will still retain the capacity for seeing the point of a story; of the story of a martyr or even the story of a monk. You will not be able rationally to read the Gospel and regard the Crucifixion as an afterthought or an anti-climax or an accident in the life of Christ; it is obviously the point of the story like the point of a sword, the sword that pierced the heart of the Mother of God.

And you will not be able rationally to read the story of a man presented as a Mirror of Christ without understanding his final phase as a Man of Sorrows, and at least artistically appreciating the appropriateness of his receiving, in a cloud of mystery and isolation, inflicted by no human hand, the unhealed everlasting wounds that heal the world.

The practical reconciliation of the gaiety and austerity I must leave the story itself to suggest. But since I have mentioned Matthew Arnold and Renan and the rationalistic admirers of St. Francis, I will here give the hint of what it seems to me most advisable for such readers to keep in mind. These distinquished writers found things like the Stigmata a stumbling-block because to them a religion was a philosophy. It was an impersonal thing; and it is only the most personal passion that provides here an approximate earthly parallel. A man will not roll in the snow for a stream of tendency by which all things fulfil the law of their being. He will not go without food in the name of something, not ourselves, that makes for righteousness. He will do things like this, or pretty nearly like this, under quite a different impulse. He will do these things when he is in love. The first fact to realise about St. Francis is involved in the first fact with which his story starts; that when he said from the first that he was a Troubadour, and said later that he was a Troubadour of a newer and nobler romance, he was not using a mere metaphor, but understood himself much better than the scholars understand him. He was, to the last agonies of asceticism, a Troubadour. He was a lover. He was a lover of God and he was really and truly a lover of men; possibly a much rarer mystical vocation. A lover of men is very nearly the opposite of a philanthropist; indeed the pedantry of the Greek word carries something like a satire on itself. A philanthropist may be said to love anthropoids. But as St. Francis did not love humanity but men, so he did not love Christianity but Christ. Say, if you think so, that he was a lunatic loving an imaginary person; but an imaginary person, not an imaginary idea. And for the modern reader the clue to the asceticism and all the rest can best be found in the stories of lovers when they seemed to be rather like lunatics. Tell it as the tale of one of the Troubadours, and the wild things he would do for his lady, and the whole of the modern puzzle disappears. In such a romance there would be no con-

tradiction between the poet gathering flowers in the
sun and enduring a freezing vigil in the snow, between his praising all earthly and bodily beauty and
then refusing to eat, between his glorifying gold and
purple and perversely going in rags, between his
showing pathetically a hunger for a happy life and
a thirst for a heroic death. All these riddles would
easily be resolved in the simplicity of any noble
love; only this was so noble a love that nine men
out of ten have hardly even heard of it. We shall see
later that this parallel of the earthly lover has a very
practical relation to the problems of his life, as to
his relations with his father and with his friends and
their families. The modern reader will almost always find that if he could only feel this kind of love
as a reality, he could feel this kind of extravagance
as a romance. But I only note it here as a preliminary point because, though it is very far from being
the final truth in the matter, it is the best approach
to it. The reader cannot even begin to see the sense
of a story that may well seem to him a very wild
one, until he understands that to this great mystic
his religion was not a thing like a theory but a thing
like a love-affair. And the only purpose of this pref-
atory chapter is to explain the limits of this present
book; which is only addressed to that part of the
modern world which finds in St. Francis a certain
modern difficulty; which can admire him yet hardly
accept him, or which can appreciate the saint almost without the sanctity. And my only claim even
to attempt such a task is that I myself have for so
long been in various stages of such a condition.
Many thousand things that I now partly comprehend I should have thought utterly incomprehensi-

ble, many things I now hold sacred I should have scouted as utterly superstitious, many things that seem to me lucid and enlightened now they are seen from the inside I should honestly have called dark and barbarous seen from the outside, when long ago in those days of boyhood my fancy first caught fire with the glory of Francis of Assisi. I too have lived in Arcady; but even in Arcady I met one walking in a brown habit who loved the woods better than Pan. The figure in the brown habit stands above the hearth in the room where I write, and alone among many such images, at no stage of my pilgrimage has he ever seemed to me a stranger. There is something of harmony between the hearth and the firelight and my own first pleasure in his words about his brother fire; for he stands far enough back in my memory to mingle with all those more domestic dreams of the first days. Even the fantastic shadows thrown by fire make a sort of shadow pantomime that belongs to the nursery; yet the shadows were even then the shadows of his favourite beasts and birds, as he saw them, grotesque but haloed with the love of God. His Brother Wolf and Brother Sheep seemed then almost like the Br'er Fox and Br'er Rabbit of a more Christian Uncle Remus. I have come slowly to see many and more marvellous aspects of such a man, but I have never lost that one. His figure stands on a sort of bridge connecting my boyhood with my conversion to many other things; for the romance of his religion had penetrated even the rationalism of that vague Victorian time. In so far as I have had this experience, I may be able to lead others a little further along that road; but only a very little further. Nobody knows better

CHAPTER II

The World St. Francis Found

The modern innovation which has substituted journalism for history, or for that tradition that is the gossip of history, has had at least one definite effect. It has insured that everybody should only hear the end of every story. Journalists are in the habit of printing above the very last chapters of their serial stories (when the hero and heroine are just about to embrace in the last chapter, as only an unfathomable perversity prevented them from doing in the first) the rather misleading words, "You can begin this story here." But even this is not a complete parallel; for the journals do give some sort of a summary of the story, while they never give anything remotely resembling a summary of the history. Newspapers not only deal with news, but they deal with everything as if it were entirely new. Tut-ankhamen, for instance, was entirely new. It is exactly in the same fashion that we read that Admiral Bangs has been shot, which is the first intimation we have that he has ever been born. There is something singularly significant in the use which journalism

makes of its stores of biography. It never thinks of
publishing the life until it is publishing the death.
As it deals with individuals it deals with institutions
and ideas. After the Great War our public began to
be told of all sorts of nations being emancipated. It
had never been told a word about their being en-
slaved. We were called upon to judge of the justice
of the settlements, when we had never been allowed to hear of the very existence of the quarrels.
People would think it pedantic to talk about the
Serbian epics and they prefer to speak in plain ev-
ery-day modern language about the Yugo-Slavonic
international new diplomacy; and they are quite ex-
cited about something they call Czecho-Slovakia
without apparently having ever heard of Bohemia.
Things that are as old as Europe are regarded as
more recent than the very latest claims pegged out
on the prairies of America. It is very exciting; like
the last act of a play to people who have only come
into the theatre just before the curtain falls. But it
does not conduct exactly to knowing what it is all
about. To those content with the mere fact of a pis-
tol-shot or a passionate embrace, such a leisurely
manner of patronising the drama may be recom-
mended. To those tormented by a merely intellectual curiosity about who is kissing or killing
whom, and why, it is unsatisfactory.

Most modern history, especially in England, suf-
fers from the same imperfection as journalism. At
best it only tells half of the history of Christendom;
and that the second half without the first half. Men
for whom reason begins with the Revival of Learning, men for whom religion begins with the Refor-
mation, can never give a complete account of any-

thing, for they have to start with institutions whose origin they cannot explain, or generally even imagine. Just as we hear of the admiral being shot but have never heard of his being born, so we all heard a great deal about the dissolution of the monasteries, but we heard next to nothing about the creation of the monasteries. Now this sort of history would be hopelessly insufficient, even for an intelligent man who hated the monasteries. It is hopelessly insufficient in connection with institutions that many intelligent men do in a quite healthy spirit hate. For instance, it is possible that some of us have occasionally seen some mention, by our learned leader-writers, of an obscure institution called the Spanish Inquisition. Well, it really is an obscure institution, according to them and the histories they read. It is obscure because its origin is obscure. Protestant history simply begins with the horrible thing in possession, as the pantomime begins with the demon king in the goblin kitchen. It is likely enough that it was, especially towards the end, a horrible thing that might be haunted by demons; but if we say this was so, we have no notion why it was so. To understand the Spanish Inquisition it would be necessary to discover two things that we have never dreamed of bothering about; what Spain was and what an Inquisition was. The former would bring in the whole great question about the Crusade against the Moors; and by what heroic chivalry a European nation freed itself of an alien domination from Africa. The latter would bring in the whole business of the other Crusade against the Albigensians, and why men loved and hated that nihilistic vision from Asia. Unless we understand that there was in these things

originally the rush and romance of a Crusade, we
cannot understand how they came to deceive men
or drag them on towards evil. The Crusaders doubtless abused their victory, but there was a victory to
abuse. And where there is victory there is valour in
the field and popularity in the forum. There is some
sort of enthusiasm that encourages excesses or covers
faults. For instance, I for one have maintained from
very early days the responsibility of the English for
their atrocious treatment of the Irish. But it would
be quite unfair to the English to describe even the
devilry of '98 and leave out altogether all mention
of the war with Napoleon. It would be unjust to suggest that the English mind was bent on nothing but
the death of Emmett, when it was more probably
full of the glory of the death of Nelson. Unfortu-
nately '98 was very far from being the last date of
such dirty work; and only a few years ago our pol-
iticians started trying to rule by random robbing and
killing, while gently remonstrating with the Irish for
their memory of old unhappy far-off things and battles long ago. But however badly we may think of
the Black-and-Tan business, it would be unjust to
forget that most of us were not thinking of Black-
and-Tan but of khaki; and that khaki had just then
a noble and national connotation covering many
things. To write of the war in Ireland and leave out
the war against Prussia, and the English sincerity
about it, would be unjust to the English. So to talk
about the torture-engine as if it had been a hideous
toy is unjust to the Spanish. It does not tell sensibly
from the start the story of what the Spaniard did,
and why. We may concede to our contemporaries
that in any case it is not a story that ends well. We

do not insist that in their version it should begin
well. What we complain of is that in their version it
does not begin at all. They are only in at the death;
or even, like Lord Tom Noddy, too late for the hanging. It is quite true that it was sometimes more horrible than any hanging; but they only gather, so to
speak, the very ashes of the ashes; the fag-end of
the faggot.

The case of the Inquisition is here taken at random, for it is one among any number illustrating the
same thing; and not because it is especially connected with St. Francis, in whatever sense it may
have been connected with St. Dominic. It may well
be suggested later indeed that St. Francis is unintelligible, just as St. Dominic is unintelligible, unless
we do understand something of what the thirteenth
century meant by heresy and a crusade. But for the
moment I use it as a lesser example for a much
larger purpose. It is to point out that to begin the
story of St. Francis with the birth of St. Francis
would be to miss the whole point of the story, or
rather not to tell the story at all. And it is to suggest
that the modern tailforemost type of journalistic history perpetually fails us. We learn about reformers
without knowing what they had to reform, about
rebels without a notion of what they rebelled
against, of memorials that are not connected with
any memory and restorations of things that had apparently never existed before. Even at the expense
of this chapter appearing disproportionate, it is necessary to say something about the great movements
that led up to the entrance of the founder of the
Franciscans. It may seem to mean describing a
world, or even a universe, in order to describe a

man. It will inevitably mean that the world or the universe will be described with a few desperate generalisations in a few abrupt sentences. But so far from its meaning that we see a very small figure under so large a sky, it will mean that we must measure the sky before we can begin to measure the towering stature of the man.

And this phrase alone brings me to the preliminary suggestions that seem necessary before even a slight sketch of the life of St. Francis. It is necessary to realise, in however rude and elementary a fashion, into what sort of a world St. Francis entered and what has been the history of that world, at least in so far as it affected him. It is necessary to have, if only in a few sentences, a sort of preface in the form of an Outline of History, if we may borrow the phrase of Mr. Wells. In the case of Mr. Wells himself, it is evident that the distinguished novelist suffered the same disadvantage as if he had been obliged to write a novel of which he hated the hero. To write history and hate Rome, both pagan and papal, is practically to hate nearly everything that has happened. It comes very near to hating humanity on purely humanitarian grounds. To dislike both the priest and the soldier, both the laurels of the warrior and the lilies of the saint, is to suffer a division from the mass of mankind for which not all the dexterities of the finest and most flexible of modern intelligences can compensate. A much wider sympathy is needed for the historical setting of St. Francis, himself both a soldier and a saint. I will therefore conclude this chapter with a few generalisations about the world that St. Francis found.

Men will not believe because they will not

broaden their minds. As a matter of individual belief, I should of course express it by saying that they are not sufficiently catholic to be Catholic. But I am not going to discuss here the doctrinal truths of Christianity, but simply the broad historical fact of Christianity, as it might appear to a really enlightened and imaginative person even if he were not a Christian. What I mean at the moment is that the majority of doubts are made out of details. In the course of random reading a man comes across a pagan custom that strikes him as picturesque or a Christian action that strikes him as cruel; but he does not enlarge his mind sufficiently to see the main truth about pagan custom or the Christian reaction against it. Until we understand, not necessarily in detail, but in their big bulk and proportion that pagan progress and that Christian reaction, we cannot really understand the point of history at which St. Francis appears or what his great popular mission was all about.

Now everybody knows, I imagine, that the twelfth and thirteenth centuries were an awakening of the world. They were a fresh flowering of culture and the creative arts after a long spell of much sterner and even more sterile experience which we call the Dark Ages. They may be called an emancipation; they were certainly an end; an end of what may at least seem a harsher and more inhuman time. But what was it that was ended? From what was it that men were emancipated? That is where there is a real collision and point at issue between the different philosophies of history. On the merely external and secular side, it has been truly said that men awoke from a sleep; but there had been dreams in that sleep of a mystical and sometimes of a monstrous kind. In that rationalistic routine into which most modern historians have fallen, it is considered enough to say that they were emancipated from mere savage superstition and advanced towards mere civilised enlightenment. Now this is the big blunder that stands as a stumbling-block at the very beginning of our story. Anybody who supposes that the Dark Ages were plain darkness and nothing else, and that the dawn of the thirteenth century was plain daylight and nothing else, will not be able to make head or tail of the human story of St. Francis of Assisi. The truth is that the joy of St. Francis and his Jongleurs de Dieu was not merely an awakening. It was something which cannot be understood without understanding their own mystical creed. The end of the Dark Ages was not merely the end of a sleep. It was certainly not merely the end of a superstitious enslavement. It was the end of something belonging to a quite definite but quite different order of ideas.

It was the end of a penance; or, if it be preferred, a purgation. It marked the moment when a certain spiritual expiation had been finally worked out and certain spiritual diseases had been finally expelled from the system. They had been expelled by an era of asceticism, which was the only thing that could have expelled them. Christianity had entered the world to cure the world; and she had cured it in the only way in which it could be cured.

Viewed merely in an external and experimental fashion, the whole of the high civilisation of antiquity had ended in the learning of a certain lesson; that is, in its conversion to Christianity. But that lesson was a psychological fact as well as a theological faith. That pagan civilisation had indeed been a very high civilisation. It would not weaken our thesis, it might even strengthen it, to say that it was the highest that humanity ever reached. It had discovered its still unrivalled arts of poetry and plastic representation; it had discovered its own permanent political ideals; it had discovered its own clear system of logic and of language. But above all, it had discovered its own mistake.

That mistake was too deep to be ideally defined; the short-hand of it is to call it the mistake of nature-worship. It might almost as truly be called the mistake of being natural; and it was a very natural mistake. The Greeks, the great guides and pioneers of pagan antiquity, started out with the idea of something splendidly obvious and direct; the idea that if man walked straight ahead on the high road of reason and nature, he could come to no harm; especially if he was, as the Greek was, eminently enlightened and intelligent. We might be so flippant as to say that man was simply to follow his nose, so long as it was a Greek nose. And the case of the Greeks themselves is alone enough to illustrate the strange but certain fatality that attends upon this fallacy. No sooner did the Greeks themselves begin to follow their own noses and their own notion of being natural, than the queerest thing in history seems to have happened to them. It was much too queer to be an easy matter to discuss. It may be remarked that our more repulsive realists never give us the benefit of their realism. Their studies of unsavoury subjects never take note of the testimony which they bear to the truths of a traditional morality. But if we had the taste for such things, we could cite thousands of such things as part of the case for Christian morals. And an instance of this is found in the fact that nobody has written, in this sense, a real moral history of the Greeks. Nobody has seen the scale or the strangeness of the story. The wisest men in the world set out to be natural; and the most unnatural thing in the world was the very first thing they did. The immediate effect of saluting the sun and the sunny sanity of nature was a perversion spreading like a pestilence. The greatest and even the purest philosophers could not apparently avoid this low sort of lunacy. Why? It would seem simple enough for the people whose poets had conceived Helen of Troy, whose sculptors had carved the Venus of Milo, to remain healthy on the point. The truth is that people who worship health cannot remain healthy. When Man goes straight he goes crooked. When he follows his nose he manages somehow to put his nose out of joint, or even to cut off his nose to spite his face; and that in accordance with something much deeper in human nature than nature-worshippers could ever understand. It was the discovery of that deeper thing, humanly speaking, that constituted the conversion to Christianity. There is a bias in man like the bias in the bowl; and Christianity was the discovery of how to correct the bias and therefore hit the mark. There are many who will smile at the saying; but it is profoundly true to say that the glad good news brought by the Gospel was the news of original sin.

Rome rose at the expense of her Greek teachers largely because she did not entirely consent to be taught these tricks. She had a much more decent do-

mestic tradition; but she ultimately suffered from
the same fallacy in her religious tradition; which was
necessarily in no small degree the heathen tradition
of nature-worship. What was the matter with the
whole heathen civilisation was that there was nothing for the mass of men in the way of mysticism,
except that concerned with the mystery of the nameless forces of nature, such as sex and growth and
death. In the Roman Empire also, long before the
end, we find nature-worship inevitably producing
things that are against nature. Cases like that of
Nero have passed into a proverb, when Sadism sat
on a throne brazen in the broad daylight. But the
truth I mean is something much more subtle and
universal than a conventional catalogue of atrocities.
What had happened to the human imagination, as
a whole, was that the whole world was coloured by
dangerous and rapidly deteriorating passions; by
natural passions becoming unnatural passions. Thus
the effect of treating sex as only one innocent natural thing was that every other innocent natural
thing became soaked and sodden with sex. For sex
cannot be admitted to a mere equality among elementary emotions or experiences like eating and
sleeping. The moment sex ceases to be a servant it
becomes a tyrant. There is something dangerous
and disproportionate in its place in human nature,
for whatever reason; and it does really need a special purification and dedication. The modern talk
about sex being free like any other sense, about the
body being beautiful like any tree or flower, is either
a description of the Garden of Eden or a piece
of thoroughly bad psychology, of which the world
grew weary two thousand years ago.

This is not to be confused with mere self-righteous sensationalism about the wickedness of the pagan world. It was not so much that the pagan world was wicked as that it was good enough to realise that its paganism was becoming wicked, or rather was on the logical high road to wickedness. I mean that there was no future for "natural magic"; to deepen it was only to darken it into black magic. There was no future for it; because in the past it had only been innocent because it was young. We might say it had only been innocent because it was shallow. Pagans were wiser than paganism; that is why the pagans became Christians. Thousands of them had philosophy and family virtues and military honour to hold them up; but by this time the purely popular thing called religion was certainly dragging them down. When this reaction against the evil is allowed for, it is true to repeat that it was an evil that was everywhere. In another and more literal sense its name was Pan.

It was no metaphor to say that these people needed a new heaven and a new earth; for they had really defiled their own earth and even their own heaven. How could their case be met by looking at the sky, when erotic legends were scrawled in stars across it; how could they learn anything from the love of birds and flowers after the sort of love stories that were told of them? It is impossible here to multiply evidences, and one small example may stand for the rest. We know what sort of sentimental associations are called up to us by the phrase "a garden"; and how we think mostly of the memory of melancholy and innocent romances, or quite as often of some gracious maiden lady or kindly old

parson pottering under a yew hedge, perhaps in
sight of a village spire. Then, let any one who knows
a little Latin poetry recall suddenly what would
once have stood in place of the sun-dial or the foun-
tain, obscene and monstrous in the sun; and of what
sort was the god of their gardens.

Nothing could purge this obsession but a religion
that was literally unearthly. It was no good telling
such people to have a natural religion full of stars
and flowers; there was not a flower or even a star
that had not been stained. They had to go into the
desert where they could find no flowers or even into
the cavern where they could see no stars. Into that
desert and that cavern the highest human intellect
entered for some four centuries; and it was the very
wisest thing it could do. Nothing but the stark supernatural stood up for its salvation; if God could not
save it, certainly the gods could not. The Early
Church called the gods of paganism devils; and the
Early Church was perfectly right. Whatever natural
religion may have to do with their beginnings, nothing but fiends now inhabited those hollow shrines.
Pan was nothing but panic. Venus was nothing but
venereal vice. I do not mean for a moment, of course,
that all the individual pagans were of this character
even to the end; but it was as individuals that they
differed from it. Nothing distinguishes paganism
from Christianity so clearly as the fact that the individual thing called philosophy had little or nothing to do with the social thing called religion. Anyhow it was no good to preach natural religion to
people to whom nature had grown as unnatural as
any religion. They knew much better than we do
what was the matter with them and what sort of de-

mons at once tempted and tormented them; and they wrote across that great space of history the text: "This sort goeth not out but by prayer and fasting."

Now the historic importance of St. Francis and the transition from the twelfth to the thirteenth century, lies in the fact that they marked the end of this expiation. Men at the close of the Dark Ages may have been rude and unlettered and unlearned in everything but wars with heathen tribes, more barbarous than themselves, but they were clean. They were like children; the first beginnings of their rude arts have all the clean pleasure of children. We have to conceive them in Europe as a whole living under little local governments, feudal in so far as they were a survival of fierce wars with the barbarians, often monastic and carrying a more friendly and fatherly character, still faintly imperial in so far as Rome still ruled as a great legend. But in Italy something had survived more typical of the finer spirit of antiquity; the republic. Italy was dotted with little states, largely democratic in their ideals, and often filled with real citizens. But the city no longer lay open as under the Roman peace, but was pent in high walls for defence against feudal war and all the citizens had to be soldiers. One of these stood in a steep and striking position on the wooded hills of Umbria; and its name was Assisi. Out of its deep gate under its high turrets was to come the message that was the gospel of the hour, "Your warfare is accomplished, your iniquity is pardoned." But it was out of all these fragmentary things of feudalism and freedom and remains of Roman Law that there was to rise, at the beginning of the

thirteenth century, vast and almost universal, the
mighty civilisation of the Middle Ages.

It is an exaggeration to attribute it entirely to the
inspiration of any one man, even the most original
genius of the thirteenth century. Its elementary
ethics of fraternity and fair play had never been entirely extinct and Christendom had never been anything less than Christian. The great truisms about
justice and pity can be found in the rudest monastic
records of the barbaric transition or the stiffest max-
ims of the Byzantine decline. And early in the elev-
enth and twelfth centuries a larger moral movement
had clearly begun. But what may fairly be said of
it is this, that over all those first movements there
was still something of that ancient austerity that
came from the long penitential period. It was the
twilight of morning; but it was still a grey twilight.
This may be illustrated by the mere mention of two
or three of these reforms before the Franciscan reform. The monastic institution itself, of course, was
far older than all these things; indeed it was undoubtedly almost as old as Christianity. Its counsels
of perfection had always taken the form of vows of
chastity and poverty and obedience. With these unworldly aims it had long ago civilised a great part
of the world. The monks had taught people to
plough and sow as well as to read and write; indeed
they had taught the people nearly everything that
the people knew. But it may truly be said that the
monks were severely practical, in the sense that
they were not only practical but also severe; though
they were generally severe with themselves and
practical for other people. All this early monastic
movement had long ago settled down and doubtless

often deteriorated; but when we come to the first
mediæval movements this sterner character is still
apparent. Three examples may be taken to illustrate
the point.

First, the ancient social mould of slavery was already beginning to melt. Not only was the slave
turning into the serf, who was practically free as re-
gards his own farm and family life, but many lords
were freeing slaves and serfs altogether. This was
done under the pressure of the priests; but especially it was done in the spirit of a penance. In one
sense, of course, any Catholic society must have an
atmosphere of penance; but I am speaking of that
rather sterner spirit of penance which had expiated
the excesses of paganism. There was about such res-
titutions the atmosphere of the death-bed; as many
of them doubtless were examples of death-bed re-
pentance. A very honest atheist with whom I once
debated made use of the expression, "Men have only
been kept in slavery by the fear of hell." As I
pointed out to him, if he had said that men had only
been freed from slavery by the fear of hell, he would
at least have been referring to an unquestionable
historical fact.

Another example was the sweeping reform of
Church discipline by Pope Gregory the Seventh. It
really was a reform, undertaken from the highest
motives and having the healthiest results; it con-
ducted a searching inquisition against simony or the
financial corruptions of the clergy; it insisted on a
more serious and self-sacrificing ideal for the life of
a parish priest. But the very fact that this largely
took the form of making universal the obligation of
celibacy will strike the note of something which,

however noble, would seem to many to be vaguely negative. The third example is in one sense the strongest of all. For the third example was a war; a heroic war and for many of us a holy war; but still something having all the stark and terrible responsibilities of war. There is no space here to say all that should be said about the true nature of the Crusades. Everybody knows that in the very darkest hour of the Dark Ages a sort of heresy had sprung up in Arabia and become a new religion of a military but nomadic sort, invoking the name of Mahomet. Intrinsically it had a character found in many heresies from the Moslem to the Monist. It seemed to the heretic a sane simplification of religion; while it seems to the Catholic an insane simplification of religion, because it simplifies all to a single idea and so loses the breadth and balance of Catholicism. Anyhow its objective character was that of a military danger to Christendom and Christendom had struck at the very heart of it, in seeking to reconquer the Holy Places. The great Duke Godfrey and the first Christians who stormed Jerusalem were heroes if there were ever any in the world; but they were the heroes of a tragedy.

Now I have taken these two or three examples of the earlier mediæval movements in order to note about them one general character, which refers back to the penance that followed paganism. There is something in all these movements that is bracing even while it is still bleak, like a wind blowing between the clefts of the mountains. That wind, austere and pure, of which the poet speaks, is really the spirit of the time, for it is the wind of a world that has at last been purified. To any one who can appreciate atmospheres there is something clear and clean about the atmosphere of this crude and often harsh society. Its very lusts are clean; for they have no longer any smell of perversion. Its very cruelties are clean; they are not the luxurious cruelties of the amphitheatre. They come either of a very simple horror at blasphemy or a very simple fury at insult. Gradually against this grey background beauty begins to appear, as something really fresh and delicate and above all surprising. Love returning is no longer what was once called platonic but what is still called chivalric love. The flowers and stars have recovered their first innocence. Fire and water are felt to be worthy to be the brother and sister of a saint. The purge of paganism is complete at last.

For water itself has been washed. Fire itself has been purified as by fire. Water is no longer that water into which slaves were flung to feed the fishes. Fire is no longer that fire through which children were passed to Moloch. Flowers smell no more of the forgotten garlands gathered in the garden of Priapus; stars stand no more as signs of the far frigidity of gods as cold as those cold fires. They are all like things newly made and awaiting new names, from one who shall come to name them. Neither the universe nor the earth have now any longer the old sinister significance of the world. They await a new reconciliation with man, but they are already capable of being reconciled. Man has stripped from his soul the last rag of nature-worship, and can return to nature.

While it was yet twilight a figure appeared silently and suddenly on a little hill above the city, dark against the fading darkness. For it was the end of a long and stern night, a night of vigil, not unvisited by stars. He stood with his hands lifted, as in so many statues and pictures, and about him was a burst of birds singing; and behind him was the break of day.

CHAPTER III

Francis the Fighter

According to one tale, which if not true would be none the less typical, the very name of St. Francis was not so much a name as a nickname. There would be something akin to his familiar and popular instinct in the notion that he was nicknamed very much as an ordinary schoolboy might be called "Frenchy" at school. According to this version, his name was not Francis at all but John; and his companions called him "Francesco" or "The little Frenchman" because of his passion for the French poetry of the Troubadours. The more probable story is that his mother had named him John when he was born in the absence of his father, who shortly returned from a visit to France, where his commercial success had filled him with so much enthusiasm for French taste and social usage that he gave his son the new name signifying the Frank or Frenchman. In either case the name has a certain significance, as connecting Francis from the first with what he himself regarded as the romantic fairyland of the Troubadours.

The name of the father was Pietro Bernardone
and he was a substantial citizen of the guild of the
cloth merchants in the town of Assisi. It is hard to
describe the position of such a man without some
appreciation of the position of such a guild and even
of such a town. It did not exactly correspond to anything that is meant in modern times either by a merchant or a man of business or a tradesman, or anything that exists under the conditions of capitalism.
Bernardone may have employed people but he was
not an employer; that is, he did not belong to an
employing class as distinct from an employed class.
The person we definitely hear of his employing is
his son Francis; who, one is tempted to guess, was
about the last person that any man of business would
employ if it were convenient to employ anybody
else. He was rich, as a peasant may be rich by the
work of his own family; but he evidently expected
his own family to work in a way almost as plain as
a peasant's. He was a prominent citizen, but he belonged to a social order which existed to prevent
him being too prominent to be a citizen. It kept
all such people on their own simple level, and no
prosperity connoted that escape from drudgery by
which in modern times the lad might have seemed
to be a lord or a fine gentleman or something other
than the cloth merchant's son. This is a rule that is
proved even in the exception. Francis was one of
those people who are popular with everybody in
any case; and his guileless swagger as a Troubadour
and leader of French fashions made him a sort of
romantic ringleader among the young men of the
town. He threw money about both in extravagance
and benevolence, in a way native to a man who

never, all his life, exactly understood what money was. This moved his mother to mingled exultation and exasperation and she said, as any tradesman's wife might say anywhere: "He is more like a prince than our son." But one of the earliest glimpses we have of him shows him as simply selling bales of cloth from a booth in the market; which his mother may or may not have believed to be one of the habits of princes. This first glimpse of the young man in the market is symbolic in more ways than one. An incident occurred which is perhaps the shortest and sharpest summary that could be given of certain curious things which were a part of his character, long before it was transfigured by transcendental faith. While he was selling velvet and fine embroideries to some solid merchant of the town, a beggar came imploring alms; evidently in a somewhat tactless manner. It was a rude and simple society and there were no laws to punish a starving man for expressing his need for food, such as have been established in a more humanitarian age; and the lack of any organised police permitted such persons to pester the wealthy without any great danger. But there was, I believe, in many places a local custom of the guild forbidding outsiders to interrupt a fair bargain; and it is possible that some such thing put the mendicant more than normally in the wrong. Francis had all his life a great liking for people who had been put hopelessly in the wrong. On this occasion he seems to have dealt with the double interview with rather a divided mind; certainly with distraction, possibly with irritation. Perhaps he was all the more uneasy because of the almost fastidious standard of manners that came to him quite naturally. All are agreed that politeness flowed from him from the first, like one of the public fountains in such a sunny Italian market place. He might have written among his own poems as his own motto that verse of Mr. Belloc's poem—

> "Of Courtesy, it is much less
>   Than courage of heart or holiness,
>   Yet in my walks it seems to me
>   That the grace of God is in Courtesy."

Nobody ever doubted that Francis Bernardone had courage of heart, even of the most ordinary manly and military sort; and a time was to come when there was quite as little doubt about the holiness and the grace of God. But I think that if there was one thing about which he was punctilious, it was punctiliousness. If there was one thing of which so humble a man could be said to be proud, he was proud of good manners. Only behind his perfectly natural urbanity were wider and even wilder possibilities, of which we get the first flash in this trivial incident. Anyhow Francis was evidently torn two ways with the botheration of two talkers, but finished his business with the merchant somehow; and when he had finished it, found the beggar was gone. Francis leapt from his booth, left all the bales of velvet and embroidery behind him apparently unprotected, and went racing across the market place like an arrow from the bow. Still running, he threaded the labyrinth of the narrow and crooked streets of the little town, looking for his beggar, whom he eventually discovered; and loaded that astonished mendicant with money. Then he straightened himself, so to speak, and swore before God that he would never all his life refuse help to a poor man. The sweeping simplicity of this undertaking is extremely characteristic. Never was any man so little afraid of his own promises. His life was one riot of rash vows; of rash vows that turned out right.

The first biographers of Francis, naturally alive with the great religious revolution that he wrought, equally naturally looked back to his first years chiefly for omens and signs of such a spiritual earthquake. But writing at a greater distance, we shall not decrease that dramatic effect, but rather increase it, if we realise that there was not at this time any external sign of anything particularly mystical about the young man. He had not anything of that early sense of his vocation that has belonged to some of the saints. Over and above his main ambition to win fame as a French poet, he would seem to have most often thought of winning fame as a soldier. He was born kind; he was brave in the normal boyish fashion; but he drew the line both in kindness and bravery pretty well where most boys would have drawn it; for instance, he had the human horror of leprosy of which few normal people felt any need to be ashamed. He had the love of gay and bright apparel which was inherent in the heraldic taste of mediæval times and seems altogether to have been rather a festive figure. If he did not paint the town red, he would probably have preferred to paint it all the colours of the rainbow, as in a mediæval picture. But in this story of the young man in gay garments scampering after the vanishing beggar in rags there are certain notes of his natural individuality that must be assumed from first to last.

For instance, there is the spirit of swiftness. In a

sense he continued running for the rest of his life, as he ran after the beggar. Because nearly all the errands he ran on were errands of mercy, there appeared in his portraiture a mere element of mildness which was true in the truest sense, but is easily misunderstood. A certain precipitancy was the very poise of his soul. This saint should be represented among the other saints as angels were sometimes represented in pictures of angels; with flying feet or even with feathers; in the spirit of the text that makes angels winds and messengers a flaming fire. It is a curiosity of language that courage actually means running; and some of our sceptics will no doubt demonstrate that courage really means running away. But his courage was running, in the sense of rushing. With all his gentleness, there was originally something of impatience in his impetuosity. The psychological truth about it illustrates very well the modern muddle about the word "practical." If we mean by what is practical what is most immediately practicable, we mean merely what is easiest. In that sense St. Francis was very unpractical, and his ultimate aims were very unworldly. But if we mean by practicality a preference for prompt effort and energy over doubt or delay, he was very practical indeed. Some might call him a madman, but he was the very reverse of a dreamer. Nobody would be likely to call him a man of business; but he was very emphatically a man of action. In some of his early experiments he was rather too much of a man of action; he acted too soon and was too practical to be prudent. But at every turn of his extraordinary career we shall find him flinging himself round corners in the most unexpected fashion, as when he flew through the crooked streets after the beggar.

Another element implied in the story, which was already partially a natural instinct, before it became a supernatural ideal, was something that had never perhaps been wholly lost in those little republics of mediæval Italy. It was something very puzzling to some people; something clearer as a rule to Southerners than to Northerners, and I think to Catholics than to Protestants; the quite natural assumption of the equality of men. It has nothing necessarily to do with the Franciscan love for men; on the contrary one of its merely practical tests is the equality of the duel. Perhaps a gentleman will never be fully an egalitarian until he can really quarrel with his servant. But it was an antecedent condition of the Franciscan brotherhood; and we feel it in this early and secular incident. Francis, I fancy, felt a real doubt about which he must attend to, the beggar or the merchant; and having attended to the merchant, he turned to attend to the beggar; he thought of them as two men. This is a thing much more difficult to describe, in a society from which it is absent, but it was the original basis of the whole business; it was why the popular movement arose in that sort of place and that sort of man. His imaginative magnanimity afterwards rose like a tower to starry heights that might well seem dizzy and even crazy; but it was founded on this high table-land of human equality.

I have taken this the first among a hundred tales of the youth of St. Francis, and dwelt on its significance a little, because until we have learned to look for the significance there will often seem to be little but a sort of light sentiment in telling the story. St. Francis is not a proper person to be patronised with merely "pretty" stories. There are any number of them; but they are too often used so as to be a sort of sentimental sediment of the mediæval world, instead of being, as the saint emphatically is, a challenge to the modern world. We must take his real human development somewhat more seriously; and the next story in which we get a real glimpse of it is in a very different setting. But in exactly the same way it opens, as if by accident, certain abysses of the mind and perhaps of the unconscious mind. Francis still looks more or less like an ordinary young man; and it is only when we look at him as an ordinary young man, that we realise what an extraordinary young man he must be.

War had broken out between Assisi and Perugia. It is now fashionable to say in a satirical spirit that such wars did not so much break out as go on indefinitely between the city-states of mediæval Italy. It will be enough to say here that if one of these mediæval wars had really gone on without stopping for a century, it might possibly have come within a remote distance of killing as many people as we kill in a year in one of our great modern scientific wars between our great modern industrial empires. But the citizens of the mediæval republic were certainly under the limitation of only being asked to die for the things with which they had always lived, the houses they inhabited, the shrines they venerated and the rulers and representatives they knew; and had not the larger vision calling them to die for the latest rumours about remote colonies as reported in anonymous newspapers. And if

we infer from our own experience that war para-
lysed civilisation, we must at least admit that these
warring towns turned out a number of paralytics
who go by the names of Dante and Michael Angelo,
Ariosto and Titian, Leonardo and Columbus, not to
mention Catherine of Siena and the subject of this
story. While we lament all this local patriotism as a
hubbub of the Dark Ages, it must seem a rather curious fact that about three quarters of the greatest
men who ever lived came out of these little towns
and were often engaged in these little wars. It remains to be seen what will ultimately come out of
our large towns; but there has been no sign of anything of this sort since they became large; and I have
sometimes been haunted by a fancy of my youth,
that these things will not come till there is a city wall
round Clapham and the tocsin is rung at night to
arm the citizens of Wimbledon.

Anyhow, the tocsin was rung in Assisi and the citizens armed, and among them Francis, the son of the
cloth merchant. He went out to fight with some company of lancers and in some fight or foray or other
he and his little band were taken prisoners. To me it
seems most probable that there had been some tale
of treason or cowardice about the disaster; for we
are told that there was one of the captives with
whom his fellow-prisoners flatly refused to associate
even in prison; and when this happens in such
circumstances, it is generally because the military
blame for the surrender is thrown on some individual. Anyhow, somebody noted a small but curious
thing, though it might seem rather negative than
positive. Francis, we are told, moved among his cap-
tive companions with all his characteristic courtesy

and even conviviality, "liberal and hilarious" as
somebody said of him, resolved to keep up their
spirits and his own. And when he came across the
mysterious outcast, traitor or coward or whatever he
was called, he simply treated him exactly like all the
rest, neither with coldness nor compassion, but with
the same unaffected gaiety and good fellowship. But
if there had been present in that prison some one
with a sort of second sight about the truth and trend
of spiritual things, he might have known he was in
the presence of something new and seemingly almost anarchic; a deep tide driving out to uncharted
seas of charity. For in this sense there was really
something wanting in Francis of Assisi, something to
which he was blind that he might see better and
more beautiful things. All those limits in good fellowship and good form, all those landmarks of social
life that divide the tolerable and the intolerable, all
those social scruples and conventional conditions
that are normal and even noble in ordinary men, all
those things that hold many decent societies together, could never hold this man at all. He liked as
he liked; he seems to have liked everybody, but especially those whom everybody disliked him for liking. Something very vast and universal was already
present in that narrow dungeon; and such a seer
might have seen in its darkness that red halo of
caritas caritatum which marks one saint among
saints as well as among men. He might have heard
the first whisper of that wild blessing that afterwards took the form of a blasphemy: "He listens to
those to whom God himself will not listen."

But though such a seer might have seen such a
truth, it is exceedingly doubtful if Francis himself

saw it. He had acted out of an unconscious largeness,
or in the fine mediæval phrase largesse, within himself, something that might almost have been lawless
if it had not been reaching out to a more divine law;
but it is doubtful whether he yet knew that the law
was divine. It is evident that he had not at this time
any notion of abandoning the military, still less of
adopting the monastic life. It is true that there is not,
as pacifists and prigs imagine, the least inconsistency between loving men and fighting them, if we
fight them fairly and for a good cause. But it seems
to me that there was more than this involved; that
the mind of the young man was really running towards a military morality in any case. About this
time the first calamity crossed his path in the form
of a malady which was to revisit him many times
and hamper his headlong career. Sickness made
him more serious; but one fancies it would only have
made him a more serious soldier, or even more serious about soldiering. And while he was recovering,
something rather larger than the little feuds and
raids of the Italian towns opened an avenue of adventure and ambition. The crown of Sicily, a considerable centre of controversy at the time, was apparently claimed by a certain Gauthier de Brienne,
and the Papal cause to aid which Gauthier was
called in aroused enthusiasm among a number of
young Assisians, including Francis, who proposed to
march into Apulia on the count's behalf; perhaps his
French name had something to do with it. For it
must never be forgotten that though that world was
in one sense a world of little things, it was a world of
little things concerned about great things. There
was more internationalism in the lands dotted with

tiny republics than in the huge homogeneous impenetrable national divisions of to-day. The legal authority of the Assisian magistrates might hardly reach further than a bow-shot from their high embattled city walls. But their sympathies might be with the ride of the Normans through Sicily or the palace of the Troubadours at Toulouse; with the Emperor throned in the German forests or the great Pope dying in the exile of Salerno. Above all, it must be remembered that when the interests of an age are mainly religious they must be universal. Nothing can be more universal than the universe. And there are several things about the religious position at that particular moment which modern people not unnaturally fail to realise. For one thing, modern people naturally think of people so remote as ancient people, and even early people. We feel vaguely that these things happened in the first ages of the Church. The Church was already a good deal more than a thousand years old. That is, the Church was then rather older than France is now, a great deal older than England is now. And she looked old then; almost as old as she does now; possibly older than she does now. The Church looked like great Charlemagne with the long white beard, who had already fought a hundred wars with the heathen, and in the legend was bidden by an angel to go forth and fight once more though he was two hundred years old. The Church had topped her thousand years and turned the corner of the second thousand; she had come through the Dark Ages in which nothing could be done except desperate fighting against the barbarians and the stubborn repetition of the creed. The creed was still being repeated after the victory or escape; but it is not unnatural to suppose that there was something a little monotonous about the repetition. The Church looked old then as now; and there were some who thought her dying then as now. In truth orthodoxy was not dead but it may have been dull; it is certain that some people began to think it dull. The Troubadours of the Provençal movement had already begun to take that turn or twist towards Oriental fancies and the paradox of pessimism, which always come to Europeans as something fresh when their own sanity seems to be something stale. It is likely enough that after all those centuries of hopeless war without and ruthless asceticism within, the official orthodoxy seemed to be something stale. The freshness and freedom of the first Christians seemed then as much as now a lost and almost prehistoric age of gold. Rome was still more rational than anything else; the Church was really wiser but it may well have seemed wearier than the world. There was something more adventurous and alluring, perhaps, about the mad metaphysics that had been blown across out of Asia. Dreams were gathering like dark clouds over the Midi to break in a thunder of anathema and civil war. Only the light lay on the great plain round Rome; but the light was blank and the plain was flat; and there was no stir in the still air and the immemorial silence about the sacred town.

High in the dark house of Assisi Francesco Bernardone slept and dreamed of arms. There came to him in the darkness a vision splendid with swords, patterned after the cross in the Crusading fashion, of spears and shields and helmets hung in a high armoury, all bearing the sacred sign. When he awoke

he accepted the dream as a trumpet bidding him
to the battlefield, and rushed out to take horse and
arms. He delighted in all the exercises of chivalry;
and was evidently an accomplished cavalier and
fighting man by the tests of the tournament and the
camp. He would doubtless at any time have preferred a Christian sort of chivalry; but it seems clear
that he was also in a mood which thirsted for glory,
though in him that glory would always have been
identical with honour. He was not without some
vision of that wreath of laurel which Cæsar has left
for all the Latins. As he rode out to war the great
gate in the deep wall of Assisi resounded with his
last boast, "I shall come back a great prince."

A little way along his road his sickness rose again
and threw him. It seems highly probable, in the light
of his impetuous temper, that he had ridden away
long before he was fit to move. And in the darkness
of this second and far more desolating interruption,
he seems to have had another dream in which a
voice said to him, "You have mistaken the meaning
of the vision. Return to your own town." And Francis trailed back in his sickness to Assisi, a very dismal and disappointed and perhaps even derided
figure, with nothing to do but to wait for what
should happen next. It was his first descent into a
dark ravine that is called the valley of humiliation,
which seemed to him very rocky and desolate, but
in which he was afterwards to find many flowers.

But he was not only disappointed and humiliated;
he was also very much puzzled and bewildered. He
still firmly believed that his two dreams must have
meant something; and he could not imagine what
they could possibly mean. It was while he was drift-

ing, one may even say mooning, about the streets of
Assisi and the fields outside the city wall, that an incident occurred to him which has not always been
immediately connected with the business of the
dreams, but which seems to me the obvious culmination of them. He was riding listlessly in some way-
side place, apparently in the open country, when he
saw a figure coming along the road towards him and
halted; for he saw it was a leper. And he knew instantly that his courage was challenged, not as the
world challenges, but as one would challenge who
knew the secrets of the heart of a man. What he saw
advancing was not the banner and spears of Perugia,
from which it never occurred to him to shrink; not
the armies that fought for the crown of Sicily, of
which he had always thought as a courageous man
thinks of mere vulgar danger. Francis Bernardone
saw his fear coming up the road towards him; the
fear that comes from within and not without; though
it stood white and horrible in the sunlight. For once
in the long rush of his life his soul must have stood
still. Then he sprang from his horse, knowing nothing between stillness and swiftness, and rushed on
the leper and threw his arms round him. It was the
beginning of a long vocation of ministry among
many lepers, for whom he did many services; to this
man he gave what money he could and mounted
and rode on. We do not know how far he rode, or
with what sense of the things around him; but it is
said that when he looked back, he could see no
figure on the road.

bitter by some loss of social prestige terrible to his sensitive spirit. As he did so he heard a voice saying to him, "Francis, seest thou not that my house is in ruins? Go and restore it for me."

Francis sprang up and went. To go and do something was one of the driving demands of his nature; probably he had gone and done it before he had at all thoroughly thought out what he had done. In any case what he had done was something very decisive and immediately very disastrous for his singular social career. In the coarse conventional language of the uncomprehending world, he stole. From his own enthusiastic point of view, he extended to his venerable father, Peter Bernardone, the exquisite excitement and inestimable privilege of assisting, more or less unconsciously, in the rebuilding of St. Damian's Church. In point of fact what he did was first to sell his own horse and then to go off and sell several bales of his father's cloth, making the sign of the cross over them to indicate their pious and charitable destination. Peter Bernardone did not see things in this light. Peter Bernardone indeed had not very much light to see by, so far as understanding the genius and temperament of his extraordinary son was concerned. Instead of understanding in what sort of a wind and flame of abstract appetites the lad was living, instead of simply telling him (as the priest practically did later) that he had done an indefensible thing with the best intentions, old Bernardone took up the matter in the hardest style; in a legal and literal fashion. He used absolute political powers like a heathen father, and himself put his son under lock and key as a vulgar thief. It would appear that the cry was caught up among many with whom the unlucky Francis had once been popular; and altogether, in his efforts to build up the house of God he had only succeeded in bringing his own house about his ears and lying buried under the ruins. The quarrel dragged drearily through several stages; at one time the wretched young man seems to have disappeared underground, so to speak, into some cavern or cellar where he remained huddled hopelessly in the darkness. Anyhow, it was his blackest moment; the whole world had turned over; the whole world was on top of him.

When he came out, it was only perhaps gradually that anybody grasped that something had happened. He and his father were summoned in the court of the bishop; for Francis had refused the authority of all legal tribunals. The bishop addressed some remarks to him, full of that excellent common sense which the Catholic Church keeps permanently as the background for all the fiery attitudes of her saints. He told Francis that he must unquestionably restore the money to his father; that no blessing could follow a good work done by unjust methods; and in short (to put it crudely) if the young fanatic would give back his money to the old fool, the incident would then terminate. There was a new air about Francis. He was no longer crushed, still less crawling, so far as his father was concerned; yet his words do not, I think, indicate either just indignation or wanton insult or anything in the nature of a mere continuation of the quarrel. They are rather remotely akin to mysterious utterances of his great model, "What have I to do with thee?" or even the terrible "Touch me not."

He stood up before them all and said, "Up to this time I have called Pietro Bernardone father, but now I am the servant of God. Not only the money but everything that can be called his I will restore to my father, even the very clothes he has given me." And he rent off all his garments except one; and they saw that that was a hair-shirt.

He piled the garments in a heap on the floor and tossed the money on top of them. Then he turned to the bishop, and received his blessing, like one who turns his back on society; and, according to the account, went out as he was into the cold world. Apparently it was literally a cold world at the moment, and snow was on the ground. A curious detail, very deep in its significance, I fancy, is given in the same account of this great crisis in his life. He went out half-naked in his hair-shirt into the winter woods, walking the frozen ground between the frosty trees; a man without a father. He was penniless, he was parentless, he was to all appearance without a trade or a plan or a hope in the world; and as he went under the frosty trees, he burst suddenly into song.

It was apparently noted as remarkable that the language in which he sang was French, or that Provençal which was called for convenience French. It was not his native language; and it was in his native language that he ultimately won fame as a poet; indeed St. Francis is one of the very first of the national poets in the purely national dialects of Europe. But it was the language with which all his most boyish ardours and ambitions had been identified; it was for him pre-eminently the language of romance. That it broke from him in this extraordinary extremity seems to me something at first sight very

strange and in the last analysis very significant.
What that significance was, or may well have been,
I will try to suggest in the subsequent chapter; it is
enough to indicate here that the whole philosophy
of St. Francis revolved round the idea of a new supernatural light on natural things, which meant the
ultimate recovery not the ultimate refusal of natural
things. And for the purpose of this purely narrative
part of the business, it is enough to record that while
he wandered in the winter forest in his hair-shirt,
like the very wildest of the hermits, he sang in the
tongue of the Troubadours.

Meanwhile the narrative naturally reverts to the
problem of the ruined or at least neglected church,
which had been the starting point of the saint's innocent crime and beatific punishment. That problem still predominated in his mind and was soon
engaging his insatiable activities; but they were activities of a new sort; and he made no more attempts
to interfere with the commercial ethics of the town
of Assisi. There had dawned on him one of those
great paradoxes that are also platitudes. He realised
that the way to build a church is not to become entangled in bargains and, to him, rather bewildering
questions of legal claim. The way to build a church
is not to pay for it, certainly not with somebody else's
money. The way to build a church is not even to pay
for it with your own money. The way to build a
church is to build it.

He went about by himself collecting stones. He
begged all the people he met to give him stones. In
fact he became a new sort of beggar, reversing the
parable; a beggar who asks not for bread but a
stone. Probably, as happened to him again and

again throughout his extraordinary existence, the very queerness of the request gave it a sort of popularity; and all sorts of idle and luxurious people fell in with the benevolent project, as they would have done with a bet. He worked with his own hands at the rebuilding of the church, dragging the material like a beast of burden and learning the very last and lowest lessons of toil. A vast number of stories are told about Francis at this as at every other period of his life; but for the purpose here, which is one of simplification, it is best to dwell on this definite re-entrance of the saint into the world by the low gate of manual labour. There does indeed run through the whole of his life a sort of double meaning, like his shadow thrown upon the wall. All his action had something of the character of an allegory; and it is likely enough that some leaden-witted scientific historian may some day try to prove that he himself was never anything but an allegory. It is true enough in this sense that he was labouring at a double task, and rebuilding something else as well as the church of St. Damian. He was not only discovering the general lesson that his glory was not to be in overthrowing men in battle but in building up the positive and creative monuments of peace. He was truly building up something else, or beginning to build it up; something that has often enough fallen into ruin but has never been past rebuilding; a church that could always be built anew though it had rotted away to its first foundation-stone, against which the gates of hell shall not prevail.

The next stage in his progress is probably marked by his transferring the same energies of architectural reconstruction to the little church of St. Mary

of the Angels at the Portiuncula. He had already
done something of the same kind at a church dedicated to St. Peter; and that quality in his life noted
above, which made it seem like a symbolical drama,
led many of his most devout biographers to note the
numerical symbolism of the three churches. There
was at any rate a more historical and practical symbolism about two of them. For the original church
of St. Damian afterwards became the seat of his
striking experiment of a female order, and of the
pure and spiritual romance of St. Clare. And the
church of the Portiuncula will remain for ever as
one of the great historic buildings of the world; for
it was there that he gathered the little knot of
friends and enthusiasts; it was the home of many
homeless men. At this time, however, it is not clear
that he had the definite idea of any such monastic
developments. How early the plan appeared in his
own mind it is of course impossible to say; but on
the face of events it first takes the form of a few
friends who attached themselves to him one by one
because they shared his own passion for simplicity.
The account given of the form of their dedication
is, however, very significant; for it was that of an
invocation of the simplification of life as suggested
in the New Testament. The adoration of Christ had
been a part of the man's passionate nature for a long
time past. But the imitation of Christ, as a sort of
plan or ordered scheme of life, may in that sense be
said to begin here.

The two men who have the credit, apparently, of
having first perceived something of what was hap-
pening in the world of the soul were a solid and
wealthy citizen named Bernard of Quintavalle and

a canon from a neighbouring church named Peter. It is the more to their credit because Francis, if one may put it so, was by this time wallowing in poverty and association with lepers and ragged mendicants; and these two men were men with much to give up; the one of comforts in the world and the other of ambition in the Church. Bernard, the rich burgher, did quite literally and finally sell all he had and give to the poor. Peter did even more; for he descended from a chair of spiritual authority, probably when he was already a man of mature years and therefore of fixed mental habits, to follow an extravagant young eccentric whom most people probably regarded as a maniac. What it was of which they had caught a glimpse, of which Francis had seen the glory, may be suggested later so far as it can be suggested at all. At this stage we need profess to see no more than all Assisi saw, and that something not altogether unworthy of comment. The citizens of Assisi only saw the camel go in triumph through the eye of the needle and God doing impossible things because to him all things were possible; only a priest who rent his robes like the Publican and not like the Pharisee and a rich man who went away joyful, for he had no possessions.

These three strange figures are said to have built themselves a sort of hut or den adjoining the leper hospital. There they talked to each other, in the intervals of drudgery and danger (for it needed ten times more courage to look after a leper than to fight for the crown of Sicily), in the terms of their new life, almost like children talking a secret language. Of these individual elements on their first friendship we can say little with certainty; but it is certain that they remained friends to the end. Bernard of Quintavalle occupies in the story something of the position of Sir Bedivere, "first made and latest left of Arthur's knights," for he reappears again at the right hand of the saint on his deathbed and receives some sort of special blessing. But all those things belong to another historical world and were quite remote from the ragged and fantastic trio in their tumble-down hut. They were not monks except perhaps in the most literal and archaic sense which was identical with hermits. They were, so to speak, three solitaries living together socially, but not as a society. The whole thing seems to have been intensely individual, as seen from the outside doubtless individual to the point of insanity. The stir of something that had in it the promise of a movement or a mission can first be felt as I have said in the affair of the appeal to the New Testament.

It was a sort of *sors virgiliana* applied to the Bible; a practice not unknown among Protestants though open to their criticism, one would think, as being rather a superstition of pagans. Anyhow it seems almost the opposite of searching the Scriptures to open them at random; but St. Francis certainly opened them at random. According to one story, he merely made the sign of the cross over the volume of the Gospel and opened it at three places reading three texts. The first was the tale of the rich young man whose refusal to sell all his goods was the occasion of the great paradox about the camel and the needle. The second was the commandment to the disciples to take nothing with them on their journey, neither scrip nor staff nor any money. The third was that saying, literally to be called crucial, that the

follower of Christ must also carry his cross. There
is a somewhat similar story of Francis finding one
of these texts, almost as accidentally, merely in lis-
tening to what happened to be the Gospel of the
day. But from the former version at least it would
seem that the incident occurred very early indeed
in his new life, perhaps soon after his breach with
his father; for it was after this oracle, apparently,
that Bernard, the first disciple, rushed forth and
scattered all his goods among the poor. If this be
so, it would seem that nothing followed it for the
moment except the individual ascetical life with the
hut for a hermitage. It must of course have been a
rather public sort of hermitage, but it was none the
less in a very real sense withdrawn from the world.
St. Simeon Stylites on the top of his pillar was in
one sense an exceedingly public character; but
there was something a little singular in his situation
for all that. It may be presumed that most people
thought the situation of Francis singular, that some
even thought it too singular. There was inevitably
indeed in any Catholic society something ultimate
and even subconscious that was at least capable of
comprehending it better than a pagan or puritan society could comprehend it. But we must not at this
stage, I think, exaggerate this potential public sympathy. As has already been suggested, the Church
and all its institutions had already the air of being
old and settled and sensible things, the monastic institutions among the rest. Common sense was com-
moner in the Middle Ages, I think, than in our own
rather jumpy journalistic age; but men like Francis
are not common in any age, nor are they to be fully
understood merely by the exercise of common sense.

The thirteenth century was certainly a progressive
period; perhaps the only really progressive period
in human history. But it can truly be called progressive precisely because its progress was very orderly.
It is really and truly an example of an epoch of reforms without revolutions. But the reforms were not
only progressive but very practical; and they were
very much to the advantage of highly practical institutions; the towns and the trading guilds and the
manual crafts. Now the solid men of town and guild
in the time of Francis of Assisi were probably very
solid indeed. They were much more economically
equal, they were much more justly governed in their
own economic environment, than the moderns who
struggle madly between starvation and the monopo-
list prizes of capitalism; but it is likely enough that
the majority of such citizens were as hard-headed
as peasants. Certainly the behaviour of the venerable Peter Bernardone does not indicate a delicate
sympathy with the fine and almost fanciful subtle-
ties of the Franciscan spirit. And we cannot measure
the beauty and originality of this strange spiritual
adventure, unless we have the humour and human
sympathy to put into plain words how it would have
looked to such an unsympathetic person at the time
when it happened. In the next chapter I shall make
an attempt, inevitably inadequate, to indicate the
inside of this story of the building of the three
churches and the little hut. In this chapter I have
but outlined it from the outside. And in concluding
that chapter I ask the reader to remember and realise what that story really looked like, when thus
seen from the outside. Given a critic of rather coarse
common sense, with no feeling about the inciden⁺

except annoyance, and how would the story seem to stand?

A young fool or rascal is caught robbing his father and selling goods which he ought to guard; and the only explanation he will offer is that a loud voice from nowhere spoke in his ear and told him to mend the cracks and holes in a particular wall. He then declares himself naturally independent of all powers corresponding to the police or the magistrates, and takes refuge with an amiable bishop who is forced to remonstrate with him and tell him he is wrong. He then proceeds to take off his clothes in public and practically throw them at his father; announcing at the same time that his father is not his father at all. He then runs about the town asking everybody he meets to give him fragments of buildings or building materials, apparently with reference to his old monomania about mending the wall. It may be an excellent thing that cracks should be filled up, but preferably not by somebody who is himself cracked; and architectural restoration like other things is not best performed by builders who, as we should say, have a tile loose. Finally the wretched youth relapses into rags and squalor and practically crawls away into the gutter. That is the spectacle that Francis must have presented to a very large number of his neighbours and friends.

How he lived at all must have seemed to them dubious; but presumably he already begged for bread as he had begged for building materials. But he was always very careful to beg for the blackest or worst bread he could get, for the stalest crusts or something rather less luxurious than the crumbs which the dogs eat, and which fall from the rich man's table. Thus he probably fared worse than an ordinary beggar; for the beggar would eat the best he could get and the saint ate the worst he could get. In plain fact he was ready to live on refuse; and it was probably something much uglier as an experience than the refined simplicity which vegetarians and water-drinkers would call the simple life. As he dealt with the question of food, so he apparently dealt with the question of clothing. He dealt with it, that is, upon the same principle of taking what he could get, and not even the best of what he could get. According to one story he changed clothes with a beggar; and he would doubtless have been content to change them with a scarecrow. In another version he got hold of the rough brown tunic of a peasant, but presumably only because the peasant gave him his very oldest brown tunic, which was probably very old indeed. Most peasants have few changes of clothing to give away; and some peasants are not specially inclined to give them away until it is absolutely necessary. It is said that in place of the girdle which he had flung off (perhaps with the more symbolic scorn because it probably carried the purse or wallet by the fashion of the period) he picked up a rope more or less at random, because it was lying near, and tied it round his waist. He undoubtedly meant it as a shabby expedient; rather as the very destitute tramp will sometimes tie his clothes together with a piece of string. He meant to strike the note of collecting his clothes anyhow, like rags from a succession of dustbins. Ten years later that make-shift costume was the uniform of five thousand men; and a hundred years later, in that, for a pontifical panoply, they laid great Dante in the grave.

of all. Everybody knows who the Troubadours were; everybody knows that very early in the Middle Ages, in the twelfth and early thirteenth centuries, there arose a civilisation in Southern France which threatened to rival or eclipse the rising tradition of Paris. Its chief product was a school of poetry, or rather more especially a school of poets. They were primarily love-poets, though they were often also satirists and critics of things in general. Their picturesque posture in history is largely due to the fact that they sang their own poems and often played their own accompaniments on the light musical instruments of the period; they were minstrels as well as men of letters. Allied to their love-poetry were other institutions of a decorative and fanciful kind concerned with the same theme. There was what was called the "Gay Science," the attempt to reduce to a sort of system the fine shades of flirtation and philandering. There were the things called Courts of Love, in which the same delicate subjects were dealt with with legal pomp and pedantry. There is one point in this part of the business that must be remembered in relation to St. Francis. There were manifest moral dangers in all this superb sentimentalism; but it is a mistake to suppose that its only danger of exaggeration was in the direction of sensualism. There was a strain in the southern romance that was actually an excess of spirituality; just as the pessimist heresy it produced was in one sense an excess of spirituality. The love was not always animal; sometimes it was so airy as to be almost allegorical. The reader realises that the lady is the most beautiful being that can possibly exist, only he has occasional doubts as to whether she does exist.

Dante owed something to the Troubadours; and the critical debates about his ideal woman are an excellent example of these doubts. We know that Beatrice was not his wife, but we should in any case be equally sure that she was not his mistress; and some critics have even suggested that she was nothing at all, so to speak, except his muse. This idea of Beatrice as an allegorical figure is, I believe, unsound; it would seem unsound to any man who has read the *Vita Nuova* and has been in love. But the very fact that it is possible to suggest it illustrates something abstract and scholastic in these mediæval passions. But though they were abstract passions they were very passionate passions. These men could feel almost like lovers, even about allegories and abstractions. It is necessary to remember this in order to realise that St. Francis was talking the true language of a troubadour when he said that he also had a most glorious and gracious lady and that her name was Poverty.

But the particular point to be noted here is not concerned so much with the word Troubadour as with the word Jongleur. It is especially concerned with the transition from one to the other; and for this it is necessary to grasp another detail about the poets of the Gay Science. A jongleur was not the same thing as a troubadour, even if the same man were both a troubadour and a jongleur. More often, I believe, they were separate men as well as separate trades. In many cases apparently the two men would walk the world together like companions in arms, or rather companions in arts. The jongleur was properly a joculator or jester; sometimes he was what we should call a juggler. This is the point, I imagine, of the tale about Taillefer the Jongleur at the battle of Hastings, who sang of the death of Roland while he tossed up his sword and caught it, as a juggler catches balls. Sometimes he may have been even a tumbler; like that acrobat in the beautiful legend who was called "The Tumbler of Our Lady," because he turned head over heels and stood on his head before the image of the Blessed Virgin, for which he was nobly thanked and comforted by her and the whole company of heaven. In the ordinary way, we may imagine, the troubadour would exalt the company with earnest and solemn strains of love and then the jongleur would do his turn as a sort of comic relief. A glorious mediæval romance remains to be written about two such companions wandering through the world. At any rate, if there is one place in which the true Franciscan spirit can be found outside the true Franciscan story, it is in that tale of the Tumbler of Our Lady. And when St. Francis called his followers the Jongleurs de Dieu, he meant something very like the Tumblers of Our Lady.

Somewhere in that transition from the ambition of the Troubadour to the antics of the Tumbler is hidden, as under a parable, the truth of St. Francis. Of the two minstrels or entertainers, the jester was presumably the servant or at least the secondary figure. St. Francis really meant what he said when he said he had found the secret of life in being the servant and the secondary figure. There was to be found ultimately in such service a freedom almost amounting to frivolity. It was comparable to the condition of the jongleur because it almost amounted to frivolity. The jester could be free when the knight was rigid; and it was possible to be a jester in the service which is perfect freedom. This parallel of the two poets or minstrels is perhaps the best preliminary and external statement of the Franciscan change of heart, being conceived under an image with which the imagination of the modern world has a certain sympathy. There was, of course, a great deal more than this involved; and we must endeavour however insufficiently to penetrate past the image to the idea. It is so far like the tumblers that it is really to many people a topsy-turvy idea.

Francis, at the time or somewhere about the time when he disappeared into the prison or the dark cavern, underwent a reversal of a certain psychological kind; which was really like the reversal of a complete somersault, in that by coming full circle it came back, or apparently came back, to the same normal posture. It is necessary to use the grotesque simile of an acrobatic antic, because there is hardly any other figure that will make the fact clear. But in the inward sense it was a profound spiritual revolution. The man who went into the cave was not the man who came out again; in that sense he was almost as different as if he were dead, as if he were a ghost or a blessed spirit. And the effects of this on his attitude towards the actual world were really as extravagant as any parallel can make them. He looked at the world as differently from other men as if he had come out of that dark hole walking on his hands.

If we apply this parable of Our Lady's Tumbler to the case, we shall come very near to the point of it. Now it really is a fact that any scene such as a landscape can sometimes be more clearly and

freshly seen if it is seen upside down. There have
been landscape-painters who adopted the most startling and pantomimic postures in order to look at it
for a moment in that fashion. Thus that inverted vision, so much more bright and quaint and arresting,
does bear a certain resemblance to the world which
a mystic like St. Francis sees every day. But herein
is the essential part of the parable. Our Lady's Tumbler did not stand on his head *in order* to see flowers
and trees as a clearer or quainter vision. He did not
do so; and it would never have occurred to him to
do so. Our Lady's Tumbler stood on his head to
please Our Lady. If St. Francis had done the same
thing, as he was quite capable of doing, it would
originally have been from the same motive; a motive
of a purely supernatural thought. It would be *after*
this that his enthusiasm would extend itself and give
a sort of halo to the edges of all earthly things. This
is why it is not true to represent St. Francis as a
mere romantic forerunner of the Renaissance and a
revival of natural pleasures for their own sake. The
whole point of him was that the secret of recovering
the natural pleasures lay in regarding them in the
light of a supernatural pleasure. In other words, he
repeated in his own person that historic process
noted in the introductory chapter; the vigil of asceticism which ends in the vision of a natural world
made new. But in the personal case there was even
more than this; there were elements that make the
parallel of the Jongleur or Tumbler even more ap-
propriate than this.

It may be suspected that in that black cell or cave
Francis passed the blackest hours of his life. By nature he was the sort of man who has that vanity

which is the opposite of pride; that vanity which is
very near to humility. He never despised his fellow
creatures and therefore he never despised the opinion of his fellow creatures; including the admiration
of his fellow creatures. All that part of his human
nature had suffered the heaviest and most crushing
blows. It is possible that after his humiliating return
from his frustrated military campaign he was called
a coward. It is certain that after his quarrel with his
father about the bales of cloth he was called a thief.
And even those who had sympathised most with
him, the priest whose church he had restored, the
bishop whose blessing he had received, had evidently treated him with an almost humorous amia-
bility which left only too clear the ultimate conclusion of the matter. He had made a fool of himself.
Any man who has been young, who has ridden
horses or thought himself ready for a fight, who has
fancied himself as a troubadour and accepted the
conventions of comradeship, will appreciate the
ponderous and crushing weight of that simple
phrase. The conversion of St. Francis, like the conversion of St. Paul, involved his being in some sense
flung suddenly from a horse; but in a sense it was
an even worse fall; for it was a war-horse. Anyhow,
there was not a rag of him left that was not ridicu-
lous. Everybody knew that at the best he had made
a fool of himself. It was a solid objective fact, like
the stones in the road, that he had made a fool of
himself. He saw himself as an object, very small and
distinct like a fly walking on a clear window pane;
and it was unmistakably a fool. And as he stared at
the word "fool" written in luminous letters before
him, the word itself began to shine and change.

We used to be told in the nursery that if a man were to bore a hole through the centre of the earth and climb continually down and down, there would come a moment at the centre when he would seem to be climbing up and up. I do not know whether this is true. The reason I do not know whether it is true is that I never happened to bore a hole through the centre of the earth, still less to crawl through it. If I do not know what this reversal or inversion feels like, it is because I have never been there. And this also is an allegory. It is certain that the writer, it is even possible that the reader, is an ordinary person who has never been there. We cannot follow St. Francis to that final spiritual overturn in which complete humiliation becomes complete holiness or happiness, because we have never been there. I for one do not profess to follow it any further than that first breaking down of the romantic barricades of boyish vanity, which I have suggested in the last paragraph. And even that paragraph, of course, is merely conjectural, an individual guess at what he may have felt; but he may have felt something quite different. But whatever else it was, it was so far analogous to the story of the man making a tunnel through the earth that it did mean a man going down and down until at some mysterious moment he begins to go up and up. We have never gone up like that because we have never gone down like that; we are obviously incapable of saying that it does not happen; and the more candidly and calmly we read human history, and especially the history of the wisest men, the more we shall come to the conclusion that it does happen. Of the intrinsic internal essence of the experience, I make no pretence of writing at all. But the external effect of it, for the purpose of this narrative, may be expressed by saying that when Francis came forth from his cave of vision, he was wearing the same word "fool" as a feather in his cap; as a crest or even a crown. He would go on being a fool; he would become more and more of a fool; he would be the court fool of the King of Paradise.

This state can only be represented in symbol; but the symbol of inversion is true in another way. If a man saw the world upside down, with all the trees and towers hanging head downwards as in a pool, one effect would be to emphasise the idea of *dependence*. There is a Latin and literal connection; for the very word dependence only means hanging. It would make vivid the Scriptural text which says that God has hung the world upon nothing. If St. Francis had seen, in one of his strange dreams, the town of Assisi upside down, it need not have differed in a single detail from itself except in being entirely the other way round. But the point is this: that whereas to the normal eye the large masonry of its walls or the massive foundations of its watch-towers and its high citadel would make it seem safer and more permanent, the moment it was turned over the very same weight would make it seem more helpless and more in peril. It is but a symbol; but it happens to fit the psychological fact. St. Francis might love his little town as much as before, or more than before; but the nature of the love would be altered even in being increased. He might see and love every tile on the steep roofs or every bird on the battlements; but he would see them all in a new and divine light of eternal danger and dependence. Instead of being merely proud of his strong city be-

cause it could not be moved, he would be thankful
to God Almighty that it had not been dropped; he
would be thankful to God for not dropping the
whole cosmos like a vast crystal to be shattered into
falling stars. Perhaps St. Peter saw the world so,
when he was crucified head-downwards.

It is commonly in a somewhat cynical sense that
men have said, "Blessed is he that expecteth nothing, for he shall not be disappointed." It was in a
wholly happy and enthusiastic sense that St. Francis
said, "Blessed is he who expecteth nothing, for he
shall enjoy everything." It was by this deliberate
idea of starting from zero, from the dark nothingness
of his own deserts, that he did come to enjoy even
earthly things as few people have enjoyed them;
and they are in themselves the best working example of the idea. For there is no way in which a man
can earn a star or deserve a sunset. But there is more
than this involved, and more indeed than is easily
to be expressed in words. It is not only true that the
less a man thinks of himself, the more he thinks of
his good luck and of all the gifts of God. It is also
true that he sees more of the things themselves when
he sees more of their origin; for their origin is a part
of them and indeed the most important part of them.
Thus they become more extraordinary by being explained. He has more wonder at them but less fear
of them; for a thing is really wonderful when it is
significant and not when it is insignificant; and a
monster, shapeless or dumb or merely destructive,
may be larger than the mountains, but is still in a
literal sense insignificant. For a mystic like St.
Francis the monsters had a meaning; that is, they
had delivered their message. They spoke no longer

in an unknown tongue. That is the meaning of all those stories, whether legendary or historical, in which he appears as a magician speaking the language of beasts and birds. The mystic will have nothing to do with mere mystery; mere mystery is generally a mystery of iniquity.

The transition from the good man to the saint is a sort of revolution; by which one for whom all things illustrate and illuminate God becomes one for whom God illustrates and illuminates all things. It is rather like the reversal whereby a lover might say at first sight that a lady looked like a flower, and say afterwards that all flowers reminded him of his lady. A saint and a poet standing by the same flower might seem to say the same thing; but indeed though they would both be telling the truth, they would be telling different truths. For one the joy of life is a cause of faith, for the other rather a result of faith. But one effect of the difference is that the sense of a divine dependence, which for the artist is like the brilliant levin-blaze, for the saint is like the broad daylight. Being in some mystical sense on the other side of things, he sees things go forth from the divine as children going forth from a familiar and accepted home, instead of meeting them as they come out, as most of us do, upon the roads of the world. And it is the paradox that by this privilege he is more familiar, more free and fraternal, more carelessly hospitable than we. For us the elements are like heralds who tell us with trumpet and tabard that we are drawing near the city of a great king; but he hails them with an old familiarity that is almost an old frivolity. He calls them his Brother Fire and his Sister Water.

So arises out of this almost nihilistic abyss the noble thing that is called Praise; which no one will ever understand while he identifies it with nature-worship or pantheistic optimism. When we say that a poet praises the whole creation, we commonly mean only that he praises the whole cosmos. But this sort of poet does really praise creation, in the sense of the act of creation. He praises the passage or transition from nonentity to entity; there falls here also the shadow of that archetypal image of the bridge, which has given to the priest his archaic and mysterious name. The mystic who passes through the moment when there is nothing but God does in some sense behold the beginningless beginnings in which there was really nothing else. He not only appreciates everything but the nothing of which everything was made. In a fashion he endures and answers even the earthquake irony of the Book of Job; in some sense he is there when the foundations of the world are laid, with the morning stars singing together and the sons of God shouting for joy. That is but a distant adumbration of the reason why the Franciscan, ragged, penniless, homeless and apparently hopeless, did indeed come forth singing such songs as might come from the stars of morning; and shouting, a son of God.

This sense of the great gratitude and the sublime dependence was not a phrase or even a sentiment; it is the whole point that this was the very rock of reality. It was not a fancy but a fact; rather it is true that beside it all facts are fancies. That we all depend in every detail, at every instant, as a Christian would say upon God, as even an agnostic would say upon existence and the nature of things, is not an illusion of imagination; on the contrary, it is the fundamental fact which we cover up, as with curtains, with the illusion of ordinary life. That ordinary life is an admirable thing in itself, just as imagination is an admirable thing in itself. But it is much more the ordinary life that is made of imagination than the contemplative life. He who has seen the whole world hanging on a hair of the mercy of God has seen the truth; we might almost say the cold truth. He who has seen the vision of his city upside-down has seen it the right way up.

Rossetti makes the remark somewhere, bitterly but with great truth, that the worst moment for the atheist is when he is really thankful and has nobody to thank. The converse of this proposition is also true; and it is certain that this gratitude produced, in such men as we are here considering, the most purely joyful moments that have been known to man. The great painter boasted that he mixed all his colours with brains, and the great saint may be said to mix all his thoughts with thanks. All goods look better when they look like gifts. In this sense it is certain that the mystical method establishes a very healthy external relation to everything else. But it must always be remembered that everything else has for ever fallen into a second place, in comparison with this simple fact of dependence on the divine reality. In so far as ordinary social relations have in them something that seems solid and self-supporting, some sense of being at once buttressed and cushioned; in so far as they establish sanity in the sense of security and security in the sense of self-sufficiency, the man who has seen the world hanging on a hair does have some difficulty in taking them so seriously as that. In so far as even the secular authorities and hierarchies, even the most natural superiorities and the most necessary subordinations, tend at once to put a man in his place, and to make him sure of his position, the man who has seen the human hierarchy upside down will always have something of a smile for its superiorities. In this sense the direct vision of divine reality does disturb solemnities that are sane enough in themselves. The mystic may have added a cubit to his stature; but he generally loses something of his status. He can no longer take himself for granted, merely because he can verify his own existence in a parish register or a family Bible. Such a man may have something of the appearance of the lunatic who has lost his name while preserving his nature; who straightway forgets what manner of man he was. "Hitherto I have called Pietro Bernardone father; but now I am the servant of God."

All these profound matters must be suggested in short and imperfect phrases; and the shortest statement of one aspect of this illumination is to say that it is the discovery of an infinite debt. It may seem a paradox to say that a man may be transported with joy to discover that he is in debt. But this is only because in commercial cases the creditor does not generally share the transports of joy; especially when the debt is by hypothesis infinite and therefore unrecoverable. But here again the parallel of a natural love-story of the nobler sort disposes of the difficulty in a flash. There the infinite creditor does share the joy of the infinite debtor; for indeed they are both debtors and both creditors. In other words debt and dependence do become pleasures in the

presence of unspoilt love; the word is used too
loosely and luxuriously in popular simplifications
like the present; but here the word is really the key.
It is the key of all the problems of Franciscan morality which puzzle the merely modern mind; but
above all it is the key of asceticism. It is the highest
and holiest of the paradoxes that the man who really
knows he cannot pay his debt will be for ever pay-
ing it. He will be for ever giving back what he cannot give back, and cannot be expected to give back.
He will be always throwing things away into a bottomless pit of unfathomable thanks. Men who think
they are too modern to understand this are in fact
too mean to understand it; we are most of us too
mean to practise it. We are not generous enough to
be ascetics; one might almost say not genial enough
to be ascetics. A man must have magnanimity of
surrender, of which he commonly only catches a
glimpse in first love, like a glimpse of our lost Eden.
But whether he sees it or not, the truth is in that
riddle; that the whole world has, or is, only one good
thing; and it is a bad debt.

If ever that rarer sort of romantic love, which was
the truth that sustained the Troubadours, falls out
of fashion and is treated as fiction, we may see some
such misunderstanding as that of the modern world
about asceticism. For it seems conceivable that some
barbarians might try to destroy chivalry in love, as
the barbarians ruling in Berlin destroyed chivalry
in war. If that were ever so, we should have the
same sort of unintelligent sneers and unimaginative
questions. Men will ask what selfish sort of woman
it must have been who ruthlessly exacted tribute in
the form of flowers, or what an avaricious creature

she can have been to demand solid gold in the form
of a ring; just as they ask what cruel kind of God
can have demanded sacrifice and self-denial. They
will have lost the clue to all that lovers have meant
by love; and will not understand that it was because
the thing was not demanded that it was done. But
whether or no any such lesser things will throw a
light on the greater, it is utterly useless to study a
great thing like the Franciscan movement while re-
maining in the modern mood that murmurs against
gloomy asceticism. The whole point about St. Francis of Assisi is that he certainly was ascetical and he
certainly was not gloomy. As soon as ever he had
been unhorsed by the glorious humiliation of his vision of dependence on the divine love, he flung himself into fasting and vigil exactly as he had flung
himself furiously into battle. He had wheeled his
charger clean round, but there was no halt or check
in the thundering impetuosity of his charge. There
was nothing negative about it; it was not a regimen
or a stoical simplicity of life. It was not self-denial
merely in the sense of self-control. It was as positive
as a passion; it had all the air of being as positive
as a pleasure. He devoured fasting as a man devours
food. He plunged after poverty as men have dug
madly for gold. And it is precisely the positive and
passionate quality of this part of his personality that
is a challenge to the modern mind in the whole
problem of the pursuit of pleasure. There undenia-
bly is the historical fact; and there attached to it is
another moral fact almost as undeniable. It is certain that he held on this heroic or unnatural course
from the moment when he went forth in his hair-
shirt into the winter woods to the moment when he

CHAPTER VI

The Little Poor Man

From that cavern, that was a furnace of glowing gratitude and humility, there came forth one of the strongest and strangest and most original personalities that human history has known. He was, among other things, emphatically what we call a character; almost as we speak of a character in a good novel or play. He was not only a humanist but a humourist; a humourist especially in the old English sense of a man always in his humour, going his own way and doing what nobody else would have done. The anecdotes about him have a certain biographical quality of which the most familiar example is Dr. Johnson; which belongs in another way to William Blake or to Charles Lamb. The atmosphere can only be defined by a sort of antithesis; the act is always unexpected and never inappropriate. Before the thing is said or done it cannot even be conjectured; but after it is said or done it is felt to be merely characteristic. It is surprisingly and yet inevitably individual. This quality of abrupt fitness and bewildering consistency belongs to St. Francis in a way that

marks him out from most men of his time. Men are
learning more and more of the solid social virtues of
mediæval civilisation; but those impressions are still
social rather than individual. The mediæval world
was far ahead of the modern world in its sense of the
things in which all men are at one: death and the
daylight of reason and the common conscience that
holds communities together. Its generalisations were
saner and sounder than the mad materialistic theo-
ries of to-day; nobody would have tolerated a Scho-
penhauer scorning life or a Nietzsche living only for
scorn. But the modern world is more subtle in its
sense of the things in which men are not at one;
in the temperamental varieties and differentiations
that make up the personal problems of life. All men
who can think themselves now realise that the great
schoolmen had a type of thought that was wonder-
fully clear; but it was as it were deliberately colour-
less. All are now agreed that the greatest art of the
age was the art of public buildings; the popular and
communal art of architecture. But it was not an age
for the art of portrait-painting. Yet the friends of St.
Francis have really contrived to leave behind a portrait; something almost resembling a devout and af-
fectionate caricature. There are lines and colours in
it that are personal almost to the extent of being per-
verse, if one can use the word perversity of an inversion that was also a conversion. Even among the
saints he has the air of a sort of eccentric, if one may
use the word of one whose eccentricity consisted in
always turning towards the centre.

Before resuming the narrative of his first adven-
tures, and the building of the great brotherhood
which was the beginning of so merciful a revolution,

I think it well to complete this imperfect personal portrait here; and having attempted in the last chapter a tentative description of the process, to add in this chapter a few touches to describe the result. I mean by the result the real man as he was after his first formative experiences; the man whom men met waking about on the Italian roads in his brown tunic tied with a rope. For that man, saving the grace of God, is the explanation of all that followed; men acted quite differently according to whether they had met him or not. If we see afterwards a vast tumult, an appeal to the Pope, mobs of men in brown habits besieging the seats of authority, Papal pronouncements, heretical sessions, trial and triumphant survival, the world full of a new movement, the friar a household word in every corner of Europe, and if we ask *why* all this happened, we can only approximate to any answer to our own question if we can, in some faint and indirect imaginative fashion, hear one human voice or see one human face under a hood. There is no answer except that Francis Bernardone had happened; and we must try in some sense to see what we should have seen if he had happened to us. In other words, after some groping suggestions about his life from the inside, we must again consider it from the outside; as if he were a stranger coming up the road towards us, along the hills of Umbria, between the olives or the vines.

Francis of Assisi was slight in figure with that sort of slightness which, combined with so much vivacity, gives the impression of smallness. He was probably taller than he looked; middle-sized, his biographers say; he was certainly very active and, considering what he went through, must have been tolerably tough. He was of the brownish Southern colouring, with a dark beard thin and pointed such as appears in pictures under the hoods of elves; and his eyes glowed with the fire that fretted him night and day. There is something about the description of all he said and did which suggests that, even more than most Italians, he turned naturally to a passionate pantomime of gestures. If this was so it is equally certain that with him, even more than with most Italians, the gestures were all gestures of politeness or hospitality. And both these facts, the vivacity and the courtesy, are the outward signs of something that mark him out very distinctively from many who might appear to be more of his kind than they really are. It is truly said that Francis of Assisi was one of the founders of the mediæval drama, and therefore of the modern drama. He was the very reverse of a theatrical person in the selfish sense; but for all that he was pre-eminently a dramatic person. This side of him can best be suggested by taking what is commonly regarded as a reposeful quality; what is commonly described as a love of nature. We are compelled to use the term; and it is entirely the wrong term.

St. Francis was not a lover of nature. Properly understood, a lover of nature was precisely what he was not. The phrase implies accepting the material universe as a vague environment, a sort of sentimental pantheism. In the romantic period of literature, in the age of Byron and Scott, it was easy enough to imagine that a hermit in the ruins of a chapel (preferably by moonlight) might find peace and a mild pleasure in the harmony of solemn forests and silent stars, while he pondered over some scroll or illuminated volume, about the liturgical nature of which the author was a little vague. In short, the hermit might love nature as a background. Now for St. Francis nothing was ever in the background. We might say that his mind had no background, except perhaps that divine darkness out of which the divine love had called up every coloured creature one by one. He saw everything as dramatic, distinct from its setting, not all of a piece like a picture but in action like a play. A bird went by him like an arrow; something with a story and a purpose, though it was a purpose of life and not a purpose of death. A bush could stop him like a brigand; and indeed he was as ready to welcome the brigand as the bush.

In a word, we talk about a man who cannot see the wood for the trees. St. Francis was a man who did not want to see the wood for the trees. He wanted to see each tree as a separate and almost a sacred thing, being a child of God and therefore a brother or sister of man. But he did not want to stand against a piece of stage scenery used merely as a background, and inscribed in a general fashion: "Scene; a wood." In this sense we might say that he was too dramatic for the drama. The scenery would have come to life in his comedies; the walls would really have spoken like Snout the Tinker and the trees would really have come walking to Dunsinane. Everything would have been in the foreground; and in that sense in the footlights. Everything would be in every sense a character. This is the quality in which, as a poet, he is the very opposite of a pantheist. He did not call nature his mother; he called a particular donkey his brother or a particular spar-

row his sister. If he had called a pelican his aunt or
an elephant his uncle, as he might possibly have
done, he would still have meant that they were particular creatures assigned by their Creator to particular places; not mere expressions of the evolution-
ary energy of things. That is where his mysticism is
so close to the common sense of the child. A child
has no difficulty about understanding that God made
the dog and the cat; though he is well aware that
the making of dogs and cats out of nothing is a mysterious process beyond his own imagination. But no
child would understand what you meant if you
mixed up the dog and the cat and everything else
into one monster with myriad legs and called it
nature. The child would resolutely refuse to make
head or tail of any such animal. St. Francis was a
mystic, but he believed in mysticism and not in mys-
tification. As a mystic he was the mortal enemy of
all those mystics who melt away the edges of things
and dissolve an entity into its environment. He was
a mystic of the daylight and the darkness; but not
a mystic of the twilight. He was the very contrary
of that sort of oriental visionary who is only a mystic
because he is too much of a sceptic to be a materialist. St. Francis was emphatically a realist, using
the word realist in its much more real mediæval
sense. In this matter he really was akin to the best
spirit of his age, which had just won its victory over
the nominalism of the twelfth century. In this indeed there was something symbolic in the contemporary art and decoration of his period; as in the art
of heraldry. The Franciscan birds and beasts were
really rather like heraldic birds and beasts; not in
the sense of being fabulous animals but in the sense

of being treated as if they were facts, clear and positive and unaffected by the illusions of atmosphere and perspective. In that sense he did see a bird sable on a field azure or a sheep argent on a field vert. But the heraldry of humility was richer than the heraldry of pride; for it saw all these things that God had given as something more precious and unique than the blazonry that princes and peers had only given to themselves. Indeed out of the depths of that surrender it rose higher than the highest titles of the feudal age; than the laurel of Cæsar or the Iron Crown of Lombardy. It is an example of extremes that meet, that the Little Poor Man, who had stripped himself of everything and named himself as nothing, took the same title that has been the wild vaunt of the vanity of the gorgeous Asiatic autocrat, and called himself the Brother of the Sun and Moon.

This quality, of something outstanding and even startling in things as St. Francis saw them, is here important as illustrating a character in his own life. As he saw all things dramatically, so he himself was always dramatic. We have to assume throughout, needless to say, that he was a poet and can only be understood as a poet. But he had one poetic privilege denied to most poets. In that respect indeed he might be called the one happy poet among all the unhappy poets of the world. He was a poet whose whole life was a poem. He was not so much a minstrel merely singing his own songs as a dramatist capable of acting the whole of his own play. The things he said were more imaginative than the things he wrote. The things he did were more imaginative than the things he said. His whole course through life was a series of scenes in which he had a sort of perpetual luck in bringing things to a beautiful crisis. To talk about the art of living has come to sound rather artificial than artistic. But St. Francis did in a definite sense make the very act of living an art, though it was an unpremeditated art. Many of his acts will seem grotesque and puzzling to a rationalistic taste. But they were always acts and not explanations; and they always meant what he meant them to mean. The amazing vividness with which he stamped himself on the memory and imagination of mankind is very largely due to the fact that he was seen again and again under such dramatic conditions. From the moment when he rent his robes and flung them at his father's feet to the moment when he stretched himself in death on the bare earth in the pattern of the cross, his life was made up of these unconscious attitudes and unhesitating gestures. It would be easy to fill page after page with examples; but I will here pursue the method found convenient everywhere in this short sketch, and take one typical example, dwelling on it with a little more detail than would be possible in a catalogue, in the hope of making the meaning more clear. The example taken here occurred in the last days of his life, but it refers back in a rather curious fashion to the first; and rounds off the remarkable unity of that romance of religion.

The phrase about his brotherhood with the sun and moon, and with the water and the fire, occurs of course in his famous poem called the Canticle of the Creatures or the Canticle of the Sun. He sang it wandering in the meadows in the sunnier season of his own career, when he was pouring upwards into the sky all the passions of a poet. It is a supremely characteristic work, and much of St. Francis could be reconstructed from that work alone. Though in some ways the thing is as simple and straightforward as a ballad, there is a delicate instinct of differentiation in it. Notice, for instance, the sense of sex in inanimate things, which goes far beyond the arbitrary genders of a grammar. It was not for nothing that he called fire his brother, fierce and gay and strong, and water his sister, pure and clear and inviolate. Remember that St. Francis was neither encumbered nor assisted by all that Greek and Roman polytheism turned into allegory, which has been to European poetry often an inspiration, too often a convention. Whether he gained or lost by his contempt of learning, it never occurred to him to connect Neptune and the nymphs with the water or Vulcan and the Cyclops with the flame. This point exactly illustrates what has already been suggested; that, so far from being a revival of paganism, the Franciscan renascence was a sort of fresh start and first awakening after a forgetfulness of paganism. Certainly it is responsible for a certain freshness in the thing itself. Anyhow St. Francis was, as it were, the founder of a new folk-lore; but he could distinguish his mermaids from his mermen and his witches from his wizards. In short, he had to make his own mythology; but he knew at a glance the goddesses from the gods. This fanciful instinct for the sexes is not the only example of an imaginative instinct of the kind. There is just the same quaint felicity in the fact that he singles out the sun with a slightly more courtly title besides that of brother; a phrase that one king might use of another, corresponding to "Monsieur notre frère." It is like a faint half ironic shadow of the shining primacy that it had held in the pagan heavens. A bishop is said to have complained of a Nonconformist saying Paul instead of Saint Paul; and to have added, "He might at least have called him Mr. Paul." So St. Francis is free of all obligation to cry out in praise or terror on the Lord God Apollo, but in his new nursery heavens, he salutes him as Mr. Sun. Those are the things in which he has a sort of inspired infancy, only to be paralleled in nursery tales. Something of the same hazy but healthy awe makes the story of Br'er Fox and Br'er Rabbit refer respectfully to Mr. Man.

This poem, full of the mirth of youth and the memories of childhood, runs through his whole life like a refrain, and scraps of it turn up continually in the ordinary habit of his talk. Perhaps the last appearance of its special language was in an incident that has always seemed to me intensely impressive, and is at any rate very illustrative of the great manner and gesture of which I speak. Impressions of that kind are a matter of imagination and in that sense of taste. It is idle to argue about them; for it is the whole point of them that they have passed beyond words; and even when they use words, seem to be completed by some ritual movement like a blessing or a blow. So, in a supreme example, there is something far past all exposition, something like the sweeping movement and mighty shadow of a hand, darkening even the darkness of Gethsemane; "Sleep on now, and take your rest. . . ." Yet there are people who have started to paraphrase and expand the story of the Passion.

St. Francis was a dying man. We might say he was an old man, at the time this typical incident occurred; but in fact he was only prematurely old; for he was not fifty when he died, worn out with his fighting and fasting life. But when he came down from the awful asceticism and more awful revelation of Alverno, he was a broken man. As will be apparent when these events are touched on in their turn, it was not only sickness and bodily decay that may well have darkened his life; he had been recently disappointed in his main mission to end the Crusades by the conversion of Islam; he had been still more disappointed by the signs of compromise and a more political or practical spirit in his own order; he had spent his last energies in protest. At this point he was told that he was going blind. If the faintest hint has been given here of what St. Francis felt about the glory and pageantry of earth and sky, about the heraldic shape and colour and symbolism of birds and beasts and flowers, some notion may be formed of what it meant to him to go blind. Yet the remedy might well have seemed worse than the disease. The remedy, admittedly an uncertain remedy, was to cauterise the eye, and that without any anæsthetic. In other words it was to burn his living eyeballs with a red-hot iron. Many of the tortures of martyrdom, which he envied in martyrology and sought vainly in Syria, can have been no worse. When they took the brand from the furnace, he rose as with an urbane gesture and spoke as to an invisible presence: "Brother Fire, God made you beautiful and strong and useful; I pray you be courteous with me."

If there be any such thing as the art of life, it seems to me that such a moment was one of its masterpieces. Not to many poets has it been given to remember their own poetry at such a moment, still less to live one of their own poems. Even William Blake would have been disconcerted if, while he was re-reading the noble lines, "Tiger, tiger, burning bright," a real large live Bengal tiger had put his head in at the window of the cottage in Felpham, evidently with every intention of biting his head off. He might have wavered before politely saluting it, above all by calmly completing the recitation of the poem to the quadruped to whom it was dedicated. Shelley, when he wished to be a cloud or a leaf carried before the wind, might have been mildly surprised to find himself turning slowly head over heels in mid-air a thousand feet above the sea. Even Keats, knowing that his hold on life was a frail one, might have been disturbed to discover that the true, the blushful Hippocrene of which he had just partaken freely had indeed contained a drug, which really ensured that he should cease upon the midnight with no pain. For Francis there was no drug; and for Francis there was plenty of pain. But his first thought was one of his first fancies from the songs of his youth. He remembered the time when a flame was a flower, only the most glorious and gaily coloured of the flowers in the garden of God; and when that shining thing returned to him in the shape of an instrument of torture, he hailed it from afar like an old friend, calling it by the nickname which might most truly be called its Christian name.

That is only one incident out of a life of such incidents; and I have selected it partly because it shows what is meant here by that shadow of gesture there is in all his words, the dramatic gesture of the south; and partly because its special reference to courtesy covers the next fact to be noted. The popular instinct of St. Francis, and his perpetual preoccupation with the idea of brotherhood, will be entirely misunderstood if it is understood in the sense of what is often called camaraderie; the backslapping sort of brotherhood. Frequently from the enemies and too frequently from the friends of the democratic ideal, there has come a notion that this note is necessary to that ideal. It is assumed that equality means all men being equally uncivil, whereas it obviously ought to mean all men being equally civil. Such people have forgotten the very meaning and derivation of the word civility, if they do not see that to be uncivil is to be uncivic. But anyhow that was not the equality which Francis of Assisi encouraged; but an equality of the opposite kind; it was a camaraderie actually founded on courtesy.

Even in that fairy borderland of his mere fancies about flowers and animals and even inanimate things, he retained this permanent posture of a sort of deference. A friend of mine said that somebody was the sort of man who apologises to the cat. St. Francis really would have apologised to the cat. When he was about to preach in a wood full of the chatter of birds, he said, with a gentle gesture, "Little sisters, if you have now had your say, it is time that I also should be heard." And all the birds were silent; as I for one can very easily believe. In deference to my special design of making matters intelligible to average modernity, I have treated separately the subject of the miraculous powers that St. Francis most certainly possessed. But even apart from any miraculous powers, men of that magnetic sort, with that intense interest in animals, often have an extraordinary power over them. St. Francis's power was always exercised with this elaborate politeness. Much of it was doubtless a sort of symbolic joke, a pious pantomime intended to convey the vital distinction in his divine mission, that he not only loved but reverenced God in all his creatures. In this sense he had the air not only of apologising to the cat or to the birds, but of apologising to a chair for sitting on it or to a table for sitting down at it. Any one who had followed him through life merely to laugh at him, as a sort of lovable lunatic, might easily have had an impression as of a lunatic who bowed to every post or took off his hat to every tree. This was all a part of his instinct for imaginative gesture. He taught world a large part of its lesson by a sort of divine dumb alphabet. But if there was this ceremonial element even in lighter or lesser matters, its significance became far more serious in the serious work of his life, which was an appeal to humanity, or rather to human beings.

I have said that St. Francis deliberately did not see the wood for the trees. It is even more true that he deliberately did not see the mob for the men. What distinguishes this very genuine democrat from any mere demagogue is that he never either deceived or was deceived by the illusion of mass-suggestion. Whatever his taste in monsters, he never saw before him a many-headed beast. He only saw the image of God multiplied but never monotonous. To him a man was always a man and did not disappear in a dense crowd any more than in a desert. He honoured all men; that is, he not only loved but respected them all. What gave him his extraordinary personal power was this; that from the Pope to the beggar, from the sultan of Syria in his pavilion to the ragged robbers crawling out of the wood, there was never a man who looked into those brown burning eyes without being certain that Francis Bernardone was really interested in *him;* in his own inner individual life from the cradle to the grave; that he himself was being valued and taken seriously, and not merely added to the spoils of some social policy or the names in some clerical document. Now for this particular moral and religious idea there is no external expression except courtesy. Exhortation does not express it, for it is not mere abstract enthusiasm; beneficence does not express it, for it is not mere pity. It can only be conveyed by a certain grand manner which may be called good manners. We may say if we like that St. Francis, in the bare and barren simplicity of his life, had clung to one rag of luxury; the manners of a court. But whereas in a court there is one king and a hundred courtiers, in this story there was one courtier, moving among a hundred kings. For he treated the whole mob of men as a mob of kings. And this was really and truly the only attitude that will appeal to that part of man to which he wished to appeal. It cannot be done by giving gold or even bread; for it is a proverb that any reveller may fling largesse in mere scorn. It cannot even be done by giving time and attention; for any number of philanthropists and benevolent bureaucrats do such work with a scorn far more cold and horrible in their hearts. No plans or proposals or efficient rearrangements will give back to a broken man his self-respect and sense of speaking with an equal. One gesture will do it.

With that gesture Francis of Assisi moved among

men; and it was soon found to have something in it of magic and to act, in a double sense, like a charm. But it must always be conceived as a completely natural gesture; for indeed it was almost a gesture of apology. He must be imagined as moving thus swiftly through the world with a sort of impetuous politeness; almost like the movement of a man who stumbles on one knee half in haste and half in obeisance. The eager face under the brown hood was that of a man always going somewhere, as if he followed as well as watched the flight of the birds. And this sense of motion is indeed the meaning of the whole revolution that he made; for the work that has now to be described was of the nature of an earthquake or a volcano, an explosion that drove outwards with dynamic energy the forces stored up by ten centuries in the monastic fortress or arsenal and scattered all its riches recklessly to the ends of the earth. In a better sense than the antithesis commonly conveys, it is true to say that what St. Benedict had stored St. Francis scattered; but in the world of spiritual things what had been stored into the barns like grain was scattered over the world as seed. The servants of God who had been a besieged garrison became a marching army; the ways of the world were filled as with thunder with the trampling of their feet and far ahead of that ever swelling host went a man singing; as simply he had sung that morning in the winter woods, where he walked alone.

CHAPTER VII

The Three Orders

There is undoubtedly a sense in which two is company and three is none; there is also another sense in which three is company and four is none, as is proved by the procession of historic and fictitious figures moving three deep, the famous trios like the Three Musketeers or the Three Soldiers of Kipling. But there is yet another and a different sense in which four is company and three is none; if we use the word company in the vaguer sense of a crowd or a mass. With the fourth man enters the shadow of a mob; the group is no longer one of three individuals only conceived individually. That shadow of the fourth man fell across the little hermitage of the Portiuncula when a man named Egidio, apparently a poor workman, was invited by St. Francis to enter. He mingled without difficulty with the merchant and the canon who had already become the companions of Francis; but with his coming an invisible line was crossed; for it must have been felt by this time that the growth of that small group had become potentially infinite, or at least that its outline

had become permanently indefinite. It may have
been in the time of that transition that Francis had
another of his dreams full of voices; but now the
voices were a clamour of the tongues of all nations,
Frenchmen and Italians and English and Spanish
and Germans, telling of the glory of God each in
his own tongue; a new Pentecost and a happier
Babel.

Before describing the first steps he took to regu-
larise the growing group, it is well to have a rough
grasp of what he conceived that group to be. He
did not call his followers monks; and it is not clear,
at this time at least, that he even thought of them
as monks. He called them by a name which is generally rendered in English as the Friars Minor; but
we shall be much closer to the atmosphere of his
own mind if we render it almost literally as The Little Brothers. Presumably he was already resolved,
indeed, that they should take the three vows of poverty, chastity and obedience which had always been
the mark of a monk. But it would seem that he was
not so much afraid of the idea of a monk as of the
idea of an abbot. He was afraid that the great spiritual magistracies which had given even to their
holiest possessors at least a sort of impersonal and
corporate pride, would import an element of pom-
posity that would spoil his extremely and almost ex-
travagantly simple version of the life of humility.
But the supreme difference between his discipline
and the discipline of the old monastic system was
concerned, of course, with the idea that the monks
were to become migratory and almost nomadic instead of stationary. They were to mingle with the
world; and to this the more old-fashioned monk

would naturally reply by asking how they were to
mingle with the world without becoming entangled
with the world. It was a much more real question
than a loose religiosity is likely to realise; but St.
Francis had his answer to it, of his own individual
sort; and the interest of the problem is in that highly
individual answer.

The good Bishop of Assisi expressed a sort of
horror at the hard life which the Little Brothers
lived at the Portiuncula, without comforts, without
possessions, eating anything they could get and
sleeping anyhow on the ground. St. Francis an-
swered him with that curious and almost stunning
shrewdness which the unworldly can sometimes
wield like a club of stone. He said, "If we had any
possessions, we should need weapons and laws to
defend them." That sentence is the clue to the whole
policy that he pursued. It rested upon a real piece
of logic; and about that he was never anything but
logical. He was ready to own himself wrong about
anything else; but he was quite certain he was right
about this particular rule. He was only once seen
angry; and that was when there was talk of an exception to the rule.

His argument was this: that the dedicated man
might go anywhere among any kind of men, even
the worst kind of men, so long as there was nothing
by which they could hold him. If he had any ties
or needs like ordinary men, he would become like
ordinary men. St. Francis was the last man in the
world to think any the worse of ordinary men for
being ordinary. They had more affection and admiration from him than they are ever likely to have
again. But for his own particular purpose of stirring

up the world to a new spiritual enthusiasm, he saw
with a logical clarity that was quite reverse of fanatical or sentimental, that friars must not become
like ordinary men; that the salt must not lose its
savour even to turn into human nature's daily food.
And the difference between a friar and an ordinary
man was really that a friar was freer than an ordinary man. It was necessary that he should be free
from the cloister; but it was even more important
that he should be free from the world. It is perfectly
sound common sense to say that there is a sense in
which the ordinary man cannot be free from the
world; or rather ought not to be free from the world.
The feudal world in particular was one labyrinthine
system of dependence; but it was not only the feudal
world that went to make up the mediæval world
nor the mediæval world that went to make up the
whole world; and the whole world is full of this
fact. Family life as much as feudal life is in its nature a system of dependence. Modern trade unions
as much as mediæval guilds are interdependent
among themselves even in order to be independent
of others. In mediæval as in modern life, even
where these limitations do exist for the sake of liberty, they have in them a considerable element of
luck. They are partly the result of circumstances;
sometimes the almost unavoidable result of circumstances. So the twelfth century had been the age of
vows; and there was something of relative freedom
in that feudal gesture of the vow; for no man asks
vows from slaves any more than from spades. Still,
in practice, a man rode to war in support of the ancient house of the Column or behind the Great Dog
of the Stairway largely because he had been born

in a certain city or countryside. But no man need obey little Francis in the old brown coat unless he chose. Even in his relations with his chosen leader he was in one sense relatively free, compared with the world around him. He was obedient but not dependent. And he was as free as the wind, he was almost wildly free, in his relation to that world around him. The world around him was, as has been noted, a network of feudal and family and other forms of dependence. The whole idea of St. Francis was that the Little Brothers should be like little fishes who could go freely in and out of that net. They could do so precisely because they were small fishes and in that sense even slippery fishes. There was nothing that the world could hold them by; for the world catches us mostly by the fringes of our garments, the futile externals of our lives. One of the Franciscans says later, "A monk should own nothing but his harp"; meaning, I suppose, that he should value nothing but his song, the song with which it was his business as a minstrel to serenade every castle and cottage, the song of the joy of the Creator in his creation and the beauty of the brotherhood of men. In imagining the life of this sort of visionary vagabond, we may already get a glimpse also of the practical side of that asceticism which puzzles those who think themselves practical. A man had to be thin to pass always through the bars and out of the cage; he had to travel light in order to ride so fast and so far. It was the whole calculation, so to speak, of that innocent cunning, that the world was to be outflanked and outwitted by him, and be embarrassed about what to do with him. You could not threaten to starve a man who was ever striving to fast. You could not ruin him and reduce him to beggary, for he was already a beggar. There was a very lukewarm satisfaction even in beating him with a stick, when he only indulged in little leaps and cries of joy because indignity was his only dignity. You could not put his head in a halter without the risk of putting it in a halo.

But one distinction between the old monks and the new friars counted especially in the matter of practicality and especially of promptitude. The old fraternities with their fixed habitations and enclosed existence had the limitations of ordinary householders. However simply they lived there must be a certain number of cells or a certain number of beds or at least a certain cubic space for a certain number of brothers; their numbers therefore depended on their land and building material. But since a man could become a Franciscan by merely promising to take his chance of eating berries in a lane or begging a crust from a kitchen, of sleeping under a hedge or sitting patiently on a doorstep, there was no economic reason why there should not be any number of such eccentric enthusiasts within any short period of time. It must also be remembered that the whole of this rapid development was full of a certain kind of democratic optimism that really was part of the personal character of St. Francis. His very asceticism was in one sense the height of optimism. He demanded a great deal of human nature not because he despised it but rather because he trusted it. He was expecting a very great deal from the extraordinary men who followed him; but he was also expecting a good deal from the ordinary men to whom he sent them. He asked the laity for food as confidently as he asked the fraternity for fasting. But he counted on the hospitality of humanity because he really did regard every house as the house of a friend. He really did love and honour ordinary men and ordinary things; indeed we may say that he only sent out the extraordinary men to encourage men to be ordinary.

This paradox may be more exactly stated or explained when we come to deal with the very interesting matter of the Third Order, which was designed to assist ordinary men to be ordinary with an extraordinary exultation. The point at issue at present is the audacity and simplicity of the Franciscan plan for quartering its spiritual soldiery upon the population; not by force but by persuasion, and even by the persuasion of impotence. It was an act of confidence and therefore a compliment. It was completely successful. It was an example of something that clung about St. Francis always; a kind of tact that looked like luck because it was as simple and direct as a thunderbolt. There are many examples in his private relations of this sort of tactless tact; this surprise effected by striking at the heart of the matter. It is said that a young friar was suffering from a sort of sulks between morbidity and humility, common enough in youth and hero-worship, in which he had got it into his head that his hero hated or despised him. We can imagine how tactfully social diplomatists would steer clear of scenes and excitements, how cautiously psychologists would watch and handle such delicate cases. Francis suddenly walked up to the young man, who was of course secretive and silent as the grave, and said, "Be not troubled in your thoughts for you are

dear to me, and even among the number of those
who are most dear. You know that you are worthy
of my friendship and society; therefore come to me,
in confidence, whensoever you will, and from friendship learn faith." Exactly as he spoke to that morbid
boy he spoke to all mankind. He always went to the
point; he always seemed at once more right and
more simple than the person he was speaking to.
He seemed at once to be laying open his guard and
yet lunging at the heart. Something in this attitude
disarmed the world as it has never been disarmed
again. He was better than other men; he was a bene-
factor of other men; and yet he was not hated. The
world came into church by a newer and nearer
door; and by friendship it learnt faith.

It was while the little knot of people at the
Portiuncula was still small enough to gather in a
small room that St. Francis resolved on his first important and even sensational stroke. It is said that
there were only twelve Franciscans in the whole
world when he decided to march, as it were, on
Rome and found a Franciscan order. It would seem
that this appeal to remote headquarters was not
generally regarded as necessary; possibly something
could have been done in a secondary way under the
Bishop of Assisi and the local clergy. It would seem
even more probable that people thought it somewhat unnecessary to trouble the supreme tribunal
of Christendom about what a dozen chance men
chose to call themselves. But Francis was obstinate
and as it were blind on this point; and his brilliant
blindness is exceedingly characteristic of him. A
man satisfied with small things, or even in love with
small things, he yet never felt quite as we do about

the disproportion between small things and large.
He never saw things to scale in our sense, but with
a dizzy disproportion which makes the mind reel.
Sometimes it seems merely out of drawing like a
gaily coloured mediæval map; and then again it
seems to have escaped from everything like a short
cut in the fourth dimension. He is said to have made
a journey to interview the Emperor, throned among
his armies under the eagle of the Holy Roman Empire, to intercede for the lives of certain little birds.
He was quite capable of facing fifty emperors to intercede for one bird. He started out with two
companions to convert the Mahometan world. He
started out with eleven companions to ask the Pope
to make a new monastic world.

Innocent III, the great Pope, according to Bonaventura, was walking on the terrace of St. John
Lateran, doubtless revolving the great political
questions which troubled his reign, when there appeared abruptly before him a person in peasant
costume whom he took to be some sort of shepherd.
He appears to have got rid of the shepherd with all
convenient speed; possibly he formed the opinion
that the shepherd was mad. Anyhow he thought no
more about it until, says the great Franciscan biographer, he dreamed that night a strange dream. He
fancied that he saw the whole huge ancient temple
of St. John Lateran, on whose high terraces he had
walked so securely, leaning horribly and crooked
against the sky as if all its domes and turrets were
stooping before an earthquake. Then he looked
again and saw that a human figure was holding it
up like a living caryatid; and the figure was that of
the ragged shepherd or peasant from whom he had

turned away on the terrace. Whether this be a fact or a figure it is a very true figure of the abrupt simplicity with which Francis won the attention and the favour of Rome. His first friend seems to have been the Cardinal Giovanni di San Paolo who pleaded for the Franciscan idea before a conclave of Cardinals summoned for the purpose. It is interesting to note that the doubts thrown upon it seem to have been chiefly doubts about whether the rule was not too hard for humanity, for the Catholic Church is always on the watch against excessive asceticism and its evils. Probably they meant, especially when they said it was unduly hard, that it was unduly dangerous. For a certain element that can only be called danger is what marks the innovation as compared with older institutions of the kind. In one sense indeed the friar was almost the opposite of the monk. The value of the old monasticism had been that there was not only an ethical but an economic repose. Out of that repose had come the works for which the world will never be sufficiently grateful, the preservation of the classics, the beginning of the Gothic, the schemes of science and philosophies, the illuminated manuscripts and the coloured glass. The whole point of a monk was that his economic affairs were settled for good; he knew where he would get his supper, though it was a very plain supper. But the whole point of a friar was that he did not know where he would get his supper. There was always a possibility that he might get no supper. There was an element of what would be called romance, as of the gipsy or adventurer. But there was also an element of potential tragedy, as of the tramp or the casual labourer. So the Cardinals of the thirteenth century were filled with compassion, seeing a few men entering of their own free will that estate to which the poor of the twentieth century are daily driven by cold coercion and moved on by the police.

Cardinal San Paolo seems to have argued more or less in this manner: it may be a hard life, but after all it is the life apparently described as ideal in the Gospel; make what compromises you think wise or humane about that ideal; but do not commit yourselves to saying that men shall *not* fulfil that ideal if they can. We shall see the importance of this argument when we come to the whole of that higher aspect of the life of St. Francis which may be called the Imitation of Christ. The upshot of the discussion was that the Pope gave his verbal approval to the project and promised a more definite endorsement, if the movement should grow to more considerable proportions. It is probable that Innocent, who was himself a man of no ordinary mentality, had very little doubt that it would do so; anyhow he was not left long in doubt before it did do so. The next passage in the history of the order is simply the story of more and more people flocking to its standard; and as has already been remarked, once it had begun to grow, it could in its nature grow much more quickly than any ordinary society requiring ordinary funds and public buildings. Even the return of the twelve pioneers from their papal audience seems to have been a sort of triumphal procession. In one place in particular, it is said, the whole population of a town, men, women and children, turned out, leaving their work and wealth and homes exactly as they stood and begging to be taken into the army of God on the spot. According to the story, it was on this occasion that St. Francis first foreshadowed his idea of the Third Order which enabled men to share in the movement without leaving the homes and habits of normal humanity. For the moment it is most important to regard this story as one example of the riot of conversion with which he was already filling all the roads of Italy. It was a world of wandering; friars perpetually coming and going in all the highways and byways, seeking to ensure that any man who met one of them by chance should have a spiritual adventure. The first Order of St. Francis had entered history.

This rough outline can only be rounded off here with some description of the Second and Third Orders, though they were founded later and at separate times. The former was an order for women and owed its existence, of course, to the beautiful friendship of St. Francis and St. Clare. There is no story about which even the most sympathetic critics of another creed have been more bewildered and misleading. For there is no story that more clearly turns on that simple test which I have taken as crucial throughout this criticism. I mean that what is the matter with these critics is that they will not believe that a heavenly love can be as real as an earthly love. The moment it is treated as real, like an earthly love, their whole riddle is easily resolved. A girl of seventeen, named Clare and belonging to one of the noble families of Assisi, was filled with an enthusiasm for the conventual life; and Francis helped her to escape from her home and to take up the conventual life. If we like to put it so, he helped her to elope into the cloister, defying her parents

as he had defied his father. Indeed the scene had
many of the elements of a regular romantic elopement; for she escaped through a hole in the wall,
fled through a wood and was received at midnight
by the light of torches. Even Mrs. Oliphant, in her
fine and delicate study of St. Francis, calls it "an
incident which we can hardly record with satisfaction."

Now about that incident I will here only say this.
If it had really been a romantic elopement and the
girl had become a bride instead of a nun, practically
the whole modern world would have made her a
heroine. If the action of the Friar towards Clare had
been the action of the Friar towards Juliet, everybody would be sympathising with her exactly as
they sympathise with Juliet. It is not conclusive to
say that Clare was only seventeen. Juliet was only
fourteen. Girls married and boys fought in battles
at such early ages in mediæval times; and a girl of
seventeen in the thirteenth century was certainly
old enough to know her own mind. There cannot
be the shadow of a doubt, for any sane person considering subsequent events, that St. Clare did know
her own mind. But the point for the moment is that
modern romanticism entirely encourages such defi-
ance of parents when it is done in the name of
romantic love. For it knows that romantic love is a
reality, but it does not know that divine love is a
reality. There may have been something to be said
for the parents of Clare; there may have been something to be said for Peter Bernardone. So there may
have been a great deal to be said for the Montagues
or the Capulets; but the modern world does not
want it said; and does not say it. The fact is that as

soon as we assume for a moment as a hypothesis, what St. Francis and St. Clare assumed all the time as an absolute, that there is a direct divine relation more glorious than any romance, the story of St. Clare's elopement is simply a romance with a happy ending; and St. Francis is the St. George or knight-errant who gave it a happy ending. And seeing that some millions of men and women have lived and died treating this relation as a reality, a man is not much of a philosopher if he cannot even treat it as a hypothesis.

For the rest, we may at least assume that no friend of what is called the emancipation of women will regret the revolt of St. Clare. She did most truly, in the modern jargon, live her own life, the life that she herself wanted to lead, as distinct from the life into which parental commands and conventional arrangements would have forced her. She became the foundress of a great feminine movement which still profoundly affects the world; and her place is with the powerful women of history. It is not clear that she would have been so great or so useful if she had made a runaway match, or even stopped at home and made a *mariage de convenance*. So much any sensible man may well say considering the matter merely from the outside; and I have no intention of attempting to consider it from the inside. If a man may well doubt whether he is worthy to write a word about St. Francis, he will certainly want words better than his own to speak of the friendship of St. Francis and St. Clare. I have often remarked that the mysteries of this story are best expressed symbolically in certain silent attitudes and actions. And I know no better symbol than that found by the felicity of popular legend, which says that one night the people of Assisi thought the trees and the holy house were on fire, and rushed up to extinguish the conflagration. But they found all quiet within, where St. Francis broke bread with St. Clare at one of their rare meetings, and talked of the love of God. It would be hard to find a more imaginative image, for some sort of utterly pure and disembodied passion, than that red halo round the unconscious figures on the hill; a flame feeding on nothing and setting the very air on fire.

But if the Second Order was the memorial of such an unearthly love, the Third Order was as solid a memorial of a very solid sympathy with earthly loves and earthly lives. The whole of this feature in Catholic life, the lay orders in touch with clerical orders, is very little understood in Protestant countries and very little allowed for in Protestant history. The vision which has been so faintly suggested in these pages has never been confined to monks or even to friars. It has been an inspiration to innumerable crowds of ordinary married men and women; living lives like our own, only entirely different. That morning glory which St. Francis spread over the earth and sky has lingered as a secret sunshine under a multitude of roofs and in a multitude of rooms. In societies like ours nothing is known of such a Franciscan following. Nothing is known of such obscure followers; and if possible less is known of the well-known followers. If we imagine passing us in the street a pageant of the Third Order of St. Francis, the famous figures would surprise us more than the strange ones. For us it would be like the unmasking of some mighty secret society. There

rides St. Louis, the great king, lord of the higher justice whose scales hang crooked in favour of the poor.
There is Dante crowned with laurel, the poet who
in his life of passions sang the praises of the Lady
Poverty, whose grey garment is lined with purple
and all glorious within. All sorts of great names from
the most recent and rationalistic centuries would
stand revealed; the great Galvani, for instance, the
father of all electricity, the magician who has made
so many modern systems of stars and sounds. So
various a following would alone be enough to prove
that St. Francis had no lack of sympathy with normal men, if the whole of his own life did not prove it.

But in fact his life did prove it, and that possibly
in a more subtle sense. There is, I fancy, some truth
in the hint of one of his modern biographers, that
even his natural passions were singularly normal
and even noble, in the sense of turning towards
things not unlawful in themselves but only unlawful
for him. Nobody ever lived of whom we could less
fitly use the word "regret" than Francis of Assisi.
Though there was much that was romantic, there
was nothing in the least sentimental about his mood.
It was not melancholy enough for that. He was of
far too swift and rushing a temper to be troubled
with doubts and reconsiderations about the race he
ran; though he had any amount of self-reproach
about not running faster. But it is true, one suspects,
that when he wrestled with the devil, as every man
must to be worth calling a man, the whispers re-
ferred mostly to those healthy instincts that he
would have approved for others; they bore no resemblance to that ghastly painted paganism which
sent its demoniac courtesans to plague St. Anthony

in the desert. If St. Francis had only pleased himself, it would have been with simpler pleasures. He was moved to love rather than lust, and by nothing wilder than wedding-bells. It is suggested in that strange story of how he defied the devil by making images in the snow, and crying out that these sufficed him for a wife and family. It is suggested in the saying he used when disclaiming any security from sin, "I may yet have children"; almost as if it was of the children rather than the woman that he dreamed. And this, if it be true, gives a final touch to the truth about his character. There was so much about him of the spirit of the morning, so much that was curiously young and clean, that even what was bad in him was good. As it was said of others that the light in their body was darkness, so it may be said of this luminous spirit that the very shadows in his soul were of light. Evil itself could not come to him save in the form of a forbidden good; and he could only be tempted by a sacrament.

CHAPTER VIII

The Mirror of Christ

No man who has been given the freedom of the Faith is likely to fall into those hole-and-corner extravagances in which later degenerate Franciscans, or rather Fraticelli, sought to concentrate entirely on St. Francis as a second Christ, the creator of a new gospel. In fact any such notion makes nonsense of every motive in the man's life; for no man would reverently magnify what he was meant to rival, or only profess to follow what he existed to supplant. On the contrary, as will appear later, this little study would rather specially insist that it was really the papal sagacity that saved the great Franciscan movement for the whole world and the universal Church, and prevented it from petering out as that sort of stale and second-rate sect that is called a new religion. Everything that is written here must be understood not only as distinct from but diametrically opposed to the idolatry of the Fraticelli. The difference between Christ and St. Francis was the difference between the Creator and the creature; and certainly no creature was ever so conscious of that colossal contrast as St. Francis himself. But subject to this understanding, it is perfectly true and it is vitally important that Christ was the pattern on which St. Francis sought to fashion himself; and that at many points their human and historical lives were even curiously coincident; and above all, that compared to most of us at least St. Francis is a most sublime approximation to his Master, and, even in being an intermediary and a reflection, is a splendid and yet a merciful Mirror of Christ. And this truth suggests another, which I think has hardly been noticed; but which happens to be a highly forcible argument for the authority of Christ being continuous in the Catholic Church.

Cardinal Newman wrote in his liveliest controversial work a sentence that might be a model of what we mean by saying that his creed tends to lucidity and logical courage. In speaking of the ease with which truth may be made to look like its own shadow or sham, he said, "And if Antichrist is like Christ, Christ I suppose is like Antichrist." Mere religious sentiment might well be shocked at the end of the sentence; but nobody could object to it except the logician who said that Cæsar and Pompey were very much alike, especially Pompey. It may give a much milder shock if I say here, what most of us have forgotten, that if St. Francis was like Christ, Christ was to that extent like St. Francis. And my present point is that it is really very enlightening to realise that Christ was like St. Francis. What I mean is this; that if men find certain riddles and hard sayings in the story of Galilee, and if they find the answers to those riddles in the story of Assisi, it really does show that a secret has been handed down in

one religious tradition and no other. It shows that
the casket that was locked in Palestine can be un-
locked in Umbria; for the Church is the keeper of
the keys.

Now in truth while it has always seemed natural
to explain St. Francis in the light of Christ, it has
not occurred to many people to explain Christ in the
light of St. Francis. Perhaps the word "light" is not
here the proper metaphor; but the same truth is admitted in the accepted metaphor of the mirror. St.
Francis is the mirror of Christ rather as the moon
is the mirror of the sun. The moon is much smaller
than the sun, but it is also much nearer to us; and
being less vivid it is more visible. Exactly in the
same sense St. Francis is nearer to us, and being a
mere man like ourselves is in that sense more imagi-
nable. Being necessarily less of a mystery, he does
not, for us, so much open his mouth in mysteries.
Yet as a matter of fact, many minor things that seem
mysteries in the mouth of Christ would seem merely
characteristic paradoxes in the mouth of St. Francis.
It seems natural to reread the more remote incidents
with the help of the more recent ones. It is a truism
to say that Christ lived before Christianity; and it
follows that as a historical figure. He is a figure in
heathen history. I mean that the medium in which
He moved was not the medium of Christendom but
of the old pagan empire; and from that alone, not
to mention the distance of time, it follows that His
circumstances are more alien to us than those of an
Italian monk such as we might meet even to-day.
I suppose the most authoritative commentary can
hardly be certain of the current or conventional
weight of all His words or phrases; of which of them

would then have seemed a common allusion and
which a strange fancy. This archaic setting has left
many of the sayings standing like hieroglyphics and
subject to many and peculiar individual interpreta-
tions. Yet it is true of almost any of them that if we
simply translate them into the Umbrian dialect of
the first Franciscans, they would seem like any other
part of the Franciscan story; doubtless in one sense
fantastic, but quite familiar. All sorts of critical controversies have revolved round the passage which
bids men consider the lilies of the field and copy
them in taking no thought for the morrow. The
sceptic has alternated between telling us to be true
Christians and do it, and explaining that it is impossible to do. When he is a communist as well as an
atheist, he is generally doubtful whether to blame
us for preaching what is impracticable or for not
instantly putting it into practice. I am not going to
discuss here the point of ethics and economics; I
merely remark that even those who are puzzled at
the saying of Christ would hardly pause in accepting it as a saying of St. Francis. Nobody would be
surprised to find that he had said, "I beseech you,
little brothers, that you be as wise as Brother Daisy
and Brother Dandelion; for never do they lie awake
thinking of to-morrow, yet they have gold crowns
like kings and emperors or like Charlemagne in all
his glory." Even more bitterness and bewilderment
has arisen about the command to turn the other
cheek and to give the coat to the robber who has
taken the cloak. It is widely held to imply the
wickedness of war among nations; about which, in
itself, not a word seems to have been said. Taken
thus literally and universally, it much more clearly

implies the wickedness of all law and government. Yet there are many prosperous peacemakers who are much more shocked at the idea of using the brute force of soldiers against a powerful foreigner than they are at using the brute force of policemen against a poor fellow-citizen. Here again I am content to point out that the paradox becomes perfectly human and probable if addressed by Francis to Franciscans. Nobody would be surprised to read that Brother Juniper did then run after the thief that had stolen his hood, beseeching him to take his gown also; for so St. Francis had commanded him. Nobody would be surprised if St. Francis told a young noble, about to be admitted to his company, that so far from pursuing a brigand to recover his shoes, he ought to pursue him to make him a present of his stockings. We may like or not the atmosphere these things imply; but we know what atmosphere they do imply. We recognise a certain note as natural and clear as the note of a bird; the note of St. Francis. There is in it something of gentle mockery of the very idea of possessions; something of a hope of disarming the enemy by generosity; something of a humorous sense of bewildering the worldly with the unexpected; something of the joy of carrying an enthusiastic conviction to a logical extreme. But anyhow we have no difficulty in recognising it if we have read any of the literature of the Little Brothers and the movement that began in Assisi. It seems reasonable to infer that if it was this spirit that made such strange things possible in Umbria, it was the same spirit that made them possible in Palestine. If we hear the same unmistakable note and sense the same indescribable savour in two things at such a distance from each other, it seems natural to suppose that the case that is more remote from our experience was like the case that is closer to our experience. As the thing is explicable on the assumption that Francis was speaking to Franciscans, it is not an irrational explanation to suggest that Christ also was speaking to some dedicated band that had much the same function as Franciscans. In other words, it seems only natural to hold, as the Catholic Church has held, that these counsels of perfection were part of a particular vocation to astonish and awaken the world. But in any case it is important to note that when we do find these particular features, with their seemingly fantastic fitness, reappearing after more than a thousand years, we find them produced by the same religious system which claims continuity and authority from the scenes in which they first appeared. Any number of philosophies will repeat the platitudes of Christianity. But it is the ancient Church that can again startle the world with the paradoxes of Christianity. *Ubi Petrus ibi Franciscus.*

But if we understand that it was truly under the inspiration of his divine Master that St. Francis did these merely quaint or eccentric acts of charity, we must understand that it was under the same inspiration that he did acts of self-denial and austerity. It is clear that these more or less playful parables of the love of men were conceived after a close study of the Sermon on the Mount. But it is evident that he made an even closer study of the silent sermon on that other mountain; the mountain that was called Golgotha. Here again he was speaking the strict historical truth, when he said that in fasting or suffering humiliation he was but trying to do something of what Christ did; and here again it seems probable that as the same truth appears at the two ends of a chain of tradition, the tradition has preserved the truth. But the import of this fact at the moment affects the next phase in the personal history of the man himself.

For as it becomes clearer that his great communal scheme is an accomplished fact and past the peril of an early collapse, as it becomes evident that there already is such a thing as an Order of the Friars Minor, this more individual and intense ambition of St. Francis emerges more and more. So soon as he certainly has followers, he does not compare himself with his followers, towards whom he might appear as a master; he compares himself more and more with his Master, towards whom he appears only as a servant. This, it may be said in passing, is one of the moral and even practical conveniences of the ascetical privilege. Every other sort of superiority may be superciliousness. But the saint is never supercilious, for he is always by hypothesis in the presence of a superior. The objection to an aristocracy is that it is a priesthood without a god. But in any case the service to which St. Francis had committed himself was one which, about this time, he conceived more and more in terms of sacrifice and crucifixion. He was full of the sentiment that he had not suffered enough to be worthy even to be a distant follower of his suffering God. And this passage in his history may really be roughly summarized as the Search for Martyrdom.

This was the ultimate idea in the remarkable business of his expedition among the Saracens in Syria.

There were indeed other elements in his conception, which are worthy of more intelligent understanding than they have often received. His idea, of course, was to bring the Crusades in a double sense to their end; that is, to reach their conclusion and to achieve their purpose. Only he wished to do it by conversion and not by conquest; that is, by intellectual and not material means. The modern mind is hard to please; and it generally calls the way of Godfrey ferocious and the way of Francis fanatical. That is, it calls any moral method unpractical, when it has just called any practical method immoral. But the idea of St. Francis was far from being a fanatical or necessarily even an unpractical idea; though perhaps he saw the problem as rather too simple, lacking the learning of his great inheritor, Raymond Lully, who understood more but has been quite as little understood. The way he approached the matter was indeed highly personal and peculiar; but that was true of almost everything he did. It was in one way a simple idea, as most of his ideas were simple ideas. But it was not a silly idea; there was a great deal to be said for it and it might have succeeded. It was, of course, simply the idea that it is better to create Christians than to destroy Moslems. If Islam had been converted, the world would have been immeasurably more united and happy; for one thing, three quarters of the wars of modern history would never have taken place. It was not absurd to suppose that this might be effected, without military force, by missionaries who were also martyrs. The Church had conquered Europe in that way and may yet conquer Asia or Africa in that way. But when all this is allowed for, there is still another sense in

which St. Francis was not thinking of Martyrdom as
a means to an end, but almost as an end in itself;
in the sense that to him the supreme end was to
come closer to the example of Christ. Through all
his plunging and restless days ran the refrain: I have
not suffered enough; I have not sacrificed enough;
I am not yet worthy even of the shadow of the crown
of thorns. He wandered about the valleys of the
world looking for the hill that has the outline of a
skull.

A little while before his final departure for the
East a vast and triumphant assembly of the whole
order had been held near the Portiuncula; and
called the Assembly of the Straw Huts, from the
manner in which that mighty army encamped in the
field. Tradition says that it was on this occasion that
St. Francis met St. Dominic for the first and last
time. It also says, what is probable enough, that the
practical spirit of the Spaniard was almost appalled
at the devout irresponsibility of the Italian, who had
assembled such a crowd without organising a com-
missariat. Dominic the Spaniard was, like nearly every Spaniard, a man with the mind of a soldier. His
charity took the practical form of provision and
preparation. But, apart from the disputes about
faith which such incidents open, he probably did
not understand in this case the power of mere popularity produced by mere personality. In all his leaps
in the dark, Francis had an extraordinary faculty of
falling on his feet. The whole countryside came
down like a landslide to provide food and drink for
this sort of pious picnic. Peasants brought waggons
of wine and game; great nobles walked about doing
the work of footmen. It was a very real victory for

the Franciscan spirit of a reckless faith not only in
God but in man. Of course there is much doubt and
dispute about the whole story and the whole relation of Francis and Dominic; and the story of the
Assembly of the Straw Huts is told from the Franciscan side. But the alleged meeting is worth mentioning, precisely because it was immediately before
St. Francis set forth on his bloodless crusade that he
is said to have met St. Dominic, who has been so
much criticised for lending himself to a more bloody
one. There is no space in this little book to explain
how St. Francis, as much as St. Dominic, would
ultimately have defended the defence of Christian
unity by arms. Indeed it would need a large book
instead of a little book to develop that point alone
from its first principles. For the modern mind is
merely a blank about the philosophy of toleration;
and the average agnostic of recent times has really
had no notion of what he meant by religious liberty
and equality. He took his own ethics as self-evident
and enforced them; such as decency or the error of
the Adamite heresy. Then he was horribly shocked
if he heard of anybody else, Moslem or Christian,
taking *his* ethics as self-evident and enforcing *them;*
such as reverence or the error of the Atheist heresy.
And then he wound up by taking all this lop-sided
illogical deadlock, of the unconscious meeting the
unfamiliar, and called it the liberality of his own
mind. Mediæval men thought that if a social system
was founded on a certain idea it must fight for that
idea, whether it was as simple as Islam or as care-
fully balanced as Catholicism. Modern men really
think the same thing, as is clear when communists
attack their ideas of property. Only they do not

think it so clearly, because they have not really
thought out their idea of property. But while it is
probable that St. Francis would have reluctantly
agreed with St. Dominic that war for the truth was
right in the last resort, it is certain that St. Dominic
did enthusiastically agree with St. Francis that it was
far better to prevail by persuasion and enlightenment if it were possible. St. Dominic devoted himself much more to persuading than to persecuting;
but there was a difference in the methods simply because there was a difference in the men. About everything St. Francis did there was something that
was in a good sense childish, and even in a good
sense wilful. He threw himself into things abruptly,
as if they had just occurred to him. He made a dash
for his Mediterranean enterprise with something of
the air of a schoolboy running away to sea.

In the first act of that attempt he characteristically
distinguished himself by becoming the Patron Saint
of Stowaways. He never thought of waiting for in-
troductions or bargains or any of the considerable
backing that he already had from rich and responsible people. He simply saw a boat and threw himself into it, as he threw himself into everything else.
It has all that air of running a race which makes his
whole life read like an escapade or even literally an
escape. He lay like lumber among the cargo, with
one companion whom he had swept with him in his
rush; but the voyage was apparently unfortunate
and erratic and ended in an enforced return to Italy.
Apparently it was after this first false start that the
great reunion took place at the Portiuncula, and between this and the final Syrian journey there was
also an attempt to meet the Moslem menace by

preaching to the Moors in Spain. In Spain indeed several of the first Franciscans had already succeeded gloriously in being martyred. But the great Francis still went about stretching out his arms for such torments and desiring that agony in vain. No one would have said more readily than he that he was probably less like Christ than those others who had already found their Calvary; but the thing remained with him like a secret; the strangest of the sorrows of man.

His later voyage was more successful, so far as arriving at the scene of operations was concerned. He arrived at the headquarters of the Crusade which was in front of the besieged city of Damietta, and went on in his rapid and solitary fashion to seek the headquarters of the Saracens. He succeeded in obtaining an interview with the Sultan; and it was at that interview that he evidently offered, and as some say proceeded, to fling himself into the fire as a divine ordeal, defying the Moslem religious teachers to do the same. It is quite certain that he would have done so at a moment's notice. Indeed throwing himself into the fire was hardly more desperate, in any case, than throwing himself among the weapons and tools of torture of a horde of fanatical Mahometans and asking them to renounce Mahomet. It is said further that the Mahometan muftis showed some coldness towards the proposed competition, and that one of them quietly withdrew while it was under discussion; which would also appear credible. But for whatever reason Francis evidently returned as freely as he came. There may be something in the story of the individual impression produced on the Sultan, which the narrator represents as a sort of

secret conversion. There may be something in the
suggestion that the holy man was unconsciously pro-
tected among half-barbarous Orientals by the halo of
sanctity that is supposed in such places to surround
an idiot. There is probably as much or more in the
more generous explanation of that graceful though
capricious courtesy and compassion which mingled
with wilder things in the stately Soldans of the type
and tradition of Saladin. Finally, there is perhaps
something in the suggestion that the tale of St. Francis might be told as a sort of ironic tragedy and
comedy called The Man Who Could Not Get Killed.
Men liked him too much for himself to let him die
for his faith; and the man was received instead
of the message. But all these are only converging
guesses at a great effort that is hard to judge, because it broke off short like the beginnings of a great
bridge that might have united East and West, and
remains one of the great might-have-beens of history.

Meanwhile the great movement in Italy was making giant strides. Backed now by papal authority as
well as popular enthusiasm, and creating a kind of
comradeship among all classes, it had started a riot
of reconstruction on all sides of religious and social
life; and especially began to express itself in that enthusiasm for building which is the mark of all the
resurrections of Western Europe. There had notably
been established at Bologna a magnificent mission
house of the Friars Minor; and a vast body of them
and their sympathisers surrounded it with a chorus
of acclamation. Their unanimity had a strange interruption. One man alone in that crowd was seen to
turn and suddenly denounce the building as if it had

been a Babylonian temple; demanding indignantly
since when the Lady Poverty had thus been insulted
with the luxury of palaces. It was Francis, a wild
figure, returned from his Eastern Crusade; and it
was the first and last time that he spoke in wrath to
his children.

A word must be said later about this serious division of sentiment and policy, about which many
Franciscans, and to some extent Francis himself,
parted company with the more moderate policy
which ultimately prevailed. At this point we need
only note it as another shadow fallen upon his spirit
after his disappointment in the desert; and as in
some sense the prelude to the next phase of his
career, which is the most isolated and the most mysterious. It is true that everything about this episode
seems to be covered with some cloud of dispute,
even including its date; some writers putting it much
earlier in the narrative than this. But whether or no
it was chronologically it was certainly logically the
culmination of the story, and may best be indicated
here. I say indicated for it must be a matter of little
more than indication; the thing being a mystery both
in the higher moral and the more trivial historical
sense. Anyhow the conditions of the affair seem to
have been these. Francis and a young companion,
in the course of their common wandering, came past
a great castle all lighted up with the festivities at-
tending a son of the house receiving the honour of
knighthood. This aristocratic mansion, which took
its name from Monte Feltro, they entered in their
beautiful and casual fashion and began to give their
own sort of good news. There were some at least who
listened to the saint "as if he had been an angel of

God"; among them a gentleman named Orlando of Chiusi, who had great lands in Tuscany and who proceeded to do St. Francis a singular and somewhat picturesque act of courtesy. He gave him a mountain; a thing somewhat unique among the gifts of the world. Presumably the Franciscan rule which forbade a man to accept money had made no detailed provision about accepting mountains. Nor indeed did St. Francis accept it save as he accepted everything, as a temporary convenience rather than a personal possession; but he turned it into a sort of refuge for the eremitical rather than the monastic life; he retired there when he wished for a life of prayer and fasting which he did not ask even his closest friends to follow. This was Alverno of the Apennines, and upon its peak there rests for ever a dark cloud that has a rim or halo of glory.

What it was exactly that happened there may never be known. The matter has been, I believe, a subject of dispute among the most devout students of the saintly life as well as between such students and others of the more secular sort. It may be that St. Francis never spoke to a soul on the subject; it would be highly characteristic, and it is certain in any case that he said very little; I think he is only alleged to have spoken of it to one man. Subject however to such truly sacred doubts, I will confess that to me personally this one solitary and indirect report that has come down to us reads very like the report of something real; of some of those things that are more real than what we call daily realities. Even something as it were double and bewildering about the image seems to carry the im-

pression of an experience shaking the senses; as does
the passage in Revelation about the supernatural
creatures full of eyes. It would seem that St. Francis beheld the heavens above him occupied by a vast
winged being like a seraph spread out like a cross.
There seems some mystery about whether the
winged figure was itself crucified or in the posture
of crucifixion, or whether it merely enclosed in its
frame of wings some colossal crucifix. But it seems
clear that there was some question of the former impression; for St. Bonaventura distinctly says that St.
Francis doubted how a seraph could be crucified,
since those awful and ancient principalities were
without the infirmity of the Passion. St. Bonaventura
suggests that the seeming contradiction may have
meant that St. Francis was to be crucified as a spirit
since he could not be crucified as a man; but whatever the meaning of the vision, the general idea of it
is very vivid and overwhelming. St. Francis saw
above him, filling the whole heavens, some vast immemorial unthinkable power, ancient like the Ancient of Days, whose calm men had conceived under
the forms of winged bulls or monstrous cherubim,
and all that winged wonder was in pain like a
wounded bird. This seraphic suffering, it is said,
pierced his soul with a sword of grief and pity; it
may be inferred that some sort of mounting agony
accompanied the ecstasy. Finally after some fashion
the apocalypse faded from the sky and the agony
within subsided; and silence and the natural air
filled the morning twilight and settled slowly in the
purple chasms and cleft abysses of the Apennines.

The head of the solitary sank, amid all that relaxacollectively all the facts or fables of another aspect of the life of St. Francis; an aspect which is, I will not say more disputable, but certainly more disputed. I mean all that mass of testimony and tradition that concerns his miraculous powers and supernatural experiences, with which it would have been easy to stud and bejewel every page of the story; only that certain circumstances necessary to the conditions of this narration make it better to gather, somewhat hastily, all such jewels into a heap.

I have here adopted this course in order to make allowance for a prejudice. It is indeed to a great extent a prejudice of the past; a prejudice that is plainly disappearing in days of greater enlightenment, and especially of a greater range of scientific experiment and knowledge. But it is a prejudice that is still tenacious in many of an older generation and still traditional in many of the younger. I mean, of course, what used to be called the belief "that miracles do not happen," as I think Matthew Arnold expressed it, in expressing the standpoint of so many of our Victorian uncles and great-uncles. In other words it was the remains of that sceptical simplification by which some of the philosophers of the early eighteenth century had popularised the impression (for a very short time) that we had discovered the regulations of the cosmos like the works of a clock, of so very simple a clock that it was possible to distinguish almost at a glance what could or could not have happened in human experience. It should be remembered that these real sceptics, of the golden age of scepticism, were quite as scornful of the first fancies of science as of the lingering legends of religion. Voltaire, when he was told that a fossil fish had been found on the peaks of the Alps, laughed openly at the tale and said that some fasting monk or hermit had dropped his fish-bones there; possibly in order to effect another monkish fraud. Everybody knows by this time that science has had its revenge on scepticism. The border between the credible and the incredible has not only become once more as vague as in any barbaric twilight; but the credible is obviously increasing and the incredible shrinking. A man in Voltaire's time did not know what miracle he would next have to throw up. A man in our time does not know what miracle he will next have to swallow.

But long before these things had happened, in those days of my boyhood when I first saw the figure of St. Francis far away in the distance and drawing me even at that distance, in those Victorian days which did seriously separate the virtues from the miracles of the saints—even in those days I could not help feeling vaguely puzzled about how this method could be applied to history. Even then I did not quite understand, and even now I do not quite understand, on what principle one is to pick and choose in the chronicles of the past which seem to be all of a piece. All our knowledge of certain historical periods, and notably of the whole mediæval period, rests on certain connected chronicles written by people who are some of them nameless and all of them dead, who cannot in any case be cross-examined and cannot in some cases be corroborated. I have never been quite clear about the nature of the right by which historians accepted masses of detail from them as definitely true, and suddenly denied their truthfulness when one detail was preternatural. I do

not complain of their being sceptics; I am puzzled
about why the sceptics are not more sceptical. I can
understand their saying that these details would
never have been included in a chronicle except by
lunatics or liars; but in that case the only inference
is that the chronicle was written by liars or lunatics.
They will write for instance: "Monkish fanaticism
found it easy to spread the report that miracles
were already being worked at the tomb of Thomas
Becket." Why should they not say equally well,
"Monkish fanaticism found it easy to spread the
slander that four knights from King Henry's court
had assassinated Thomas Becket in the cathedral"?
They would write something like this: "The credulity of the age readily believed that Joan of Arc had
been inspired to point out the Dauphin although he
was in disguise." Why should they not write on the
same principle: "The credulity of the age was such
as to suppose that an obscure peasant girl could get
an audience at the court of the Dauphin"? And so,
in the present case, when they tell us there is a wild
story that St. Francis flung himself into the fire and
emerged scathless, upon what precise principle are
they forbidden to tell us of a wild story that St. Francis flung himself into the camp of the ferocious Moslems and returned safe? I only ask for information;
for I do not see the rationale of the thing myself. I
will undertake to say there was not a word written
of St. Francis by any contemporary who was himself incapable of believing and telling a miraculous
story. Perhaps it is all monkish fables and there
never was any St. Francis or any St. Thomas Becket
or any Joan of Arc. This is undoubtedly a *reductio*

ad absurdum; but it is a *reductio ad absurdum* of the view which thought all miracles absurd.

And in abstract logic this method of selection would lead to the wildest absurdities. An intrinsically incredible story could only mean that the authority was unworthy of credit. It could not mean that other parts of his story must be received with complete credulity. If somebody said he had met a man in yellow trousers, who proceeded to jump down his own throat, we should not exactly take our Bible oath or be burned at the stake for the statement that he wore yellow trousers. If somebody claimed to have gone up in a blue balloon and found that the moon was made of green cheese, we should not exactly take an affidavit that the balloon was blue any more than that the moon was green. And the really logical conclusion from throwing doubts on all tales like the miracles of St. Francis was to throw doubts on the existence of men like St. Francis. And there really was a modern moment, a sort of high-water mark of insane scepticism, when this sort of thing was really said or done. People used to go about saying that there was no such person as St. Patrick; which is every bit as much of a human and historical howler as saying there was no such person as St. Francis. There was a time, for instance, when the madness of mythological explanation had dissolved a large part of solid history under the universal and luxuriant warmth and radiance of the Sun-Myth. I believe that that particular sun has already set, but there have been any number of moons and meteors to take its place.

St. Francis, of course, would make a magnificent Sun-Myth. How could anybody miss the chance of

being a Sun-Myth when he is actually best known
by a song called The Canticle of the Sun? It is needless to point out that the fire in Syria was the dawn
in the East and the bleeding wounds in Tuscany the
sunset in the West. I could expound this theory at
considerable length; only, as so often happens to
such fine theorists, another and more promising theory occurs to me. I cannot think how everybody, including myself, can have overlooked the fact that
the whole tale of St. Francis is of Totemistic origin.
It is unquestionably a tale that simply swarms with
totems. The Franciscan woods are as full of them as
any Red Indian fable. Francis is made to call himself
an ass, because in the original mythos Francis was
merely the name given to the real four-footed donkey, afterwards vaguely evolved into a half-human
god or hero. And that, no doubt, is why I used to
feel that the Brother Wolf and Sister Bird of St.
Francis were somehow like the Br'er Fox and Sis
Cow of Uncle Remus. Some say there is an innocent
stage of infancy in which we do really believe that
a cow talked or a fox made a tar baby. Anyhow
there is an innocent period of intellectual growth in
which we do sometimes really believe that St.
Patrick was a Sun-Myth or St. Francis a Totem. But
for the most of us both those phases of paradise are
past.

As I shall suggest in a moment, there is one sense
in which we can for practical purposes distinguish
between probable and improbable things in such a
story. It is not so much a question of cosmic criticism
about the nature of the event as of literary criticism
about the nature of the story. Some stories are told
much more seriously than others. But apart from

this, I shall not attempt here any definite differentiation between them. I shall not do so for a practical reason affecting the utility of the proceeding; I mean the fact that in a practical sense the whole of this matter is again in the melting pot, from which many things may emerge moulded into what rationalism would have called monsters. The fixed points of faith and philosophy do indeed remain always the same. Whether a man believes that fire in one case could fail to burn depends on why he thinks it generally does burn. If it burns nine sticks out of ten because it is its nature or doom to do so, then it will burn the tenth stick as well. If it burns nine sticks because it is the will of God that it should, then it might be the will of God that the tenth should be unburned. Nobody can get behind that fundamental difference about the reason of things; and it is as rational for a theist to believe in miracles as for an atheist to disbelieve in them. In other words there is only one intelligent reason why a man does not believe in miracles and that is that he does believe in materialism. But these fixed points of faith and philosophy are things for a theoretical work and have no particular place here. And in the matter of history and biography, which have their place here, nothing is fixed at all. The world is in a welter of the possible and impossible, and nobody knows what will be the next scientific hypothesis to support some ancient superstition. Three-quarters of the miracles attributed to St. Francis would already be explained by psychologists, not indeed as a Catholic explains them, but as a materialist must necessarily refuse to explain them. There is one whole department of the miracles of St. Francis; the mira-

cles of healing. What is the good of a superior sceptic throwing them away as unthinkable, at the
moment when faith-healing is already a big boom-
ing Yankee business like Barnum's Show? There is
another whole department analogous to the tales of
Christ "perceiving men's thoughts." What is the use
of censoring them and blacking them out because
they are marked "miracles," when thought-reading
is already a parlour game like musical chairs? There
is another whole department, to be studied separately if such scientific study were possible, of the
well-attested wonders worked from his relics and
fragmentary possessions. What is the use of dismiss-
ing all that as inconceivable, when even these common psychical parlour tricks turn perpetually upon
touching some familiar object or holding in the hand
some personal possession? I do not believe, of course,
that these tricks are of the same type as the good
works of the saint; save perhaps in the sense of *Di-
abolus simius Dei*. But it is not a question of what
I believe and why, but of what the sceptic disbe-
lieves and why. And the moral for the practical
biographer and historian is that he must wait till
things settle down a little more, before he claims to
disbelieve anything.

This being so he can choose between two courses;
and not without some hesitation, I have here chosen
between them. The best and boldest course would
be to tell the whole story in a straightforward way,
miracles and all, as the original historians told it.
And to this sane and simple course the new historians will probably have to return. But it must be
remembered that this book is avowedly only an introduction to St. Francis or the study of St. Francis.

Those who need an introduction are in their nature strangers. With them the object is to get them to listen to St. Francis at all; and in doing so it is perfectly legitimate so to arrange the order of the facts that the familiar come before the unfamiliar and those they can at once understand before those they have a difficulty in understanding. I should only be too thankful if this thin and scratchy sketch contains a line or two that attracts men to study St. Francis for themselves; and if they do study him for themselves, they will soon find that the supernatural part of the story seems quite as natural as the rest. But it was necessary that my outline should be a merely human one, since I was only presenting his claim on all humanity, including sceptical humanity. I therefore adopted the alternative course, of showing first that nobody but a born fool could fail to realise that Francis of Assisi was a very real historical human being; and then summarising briefly in this chapter the superhuman powers that were certainly a part of that history and humanity. It only remains to say a few words about some distinctions that may reasonably be observed in the matter by any man of any views; that he may not confuse the point and climax of the saint's life with the fancies or rumours that were really only the fringes of his reputation.

There is so immense a mass of legends and anecdotes about St. Francis of Assisi, and there are so many admirable compilations that cover nearly all of them, that I have been compelled within these narrow limits to pursue a somewhat narrow policy; that of following one line of explanation and only mentioning one anecdote here or there because it illustrates that explanation. If this is true about all the legends and stories, it is especially true about the miraculous legends and the supernatural stories. If we were to take some stories as they stand, we should receive a rather bewildered impression that the biography contains more supernatural events than natural ones. Now it is clean against Catholic tradition, co-incident in so many points with common sense, to suppose that this is really the proportion of these things in practical human life. Moreover, even considered as supernatural or preternatural stories, they obviously fall into certain different classes, not so much by our experience of miracles as by our experience of stories. Some of them have the character of fairy stories in their form even more than their incident. They are obviously tales told by the fire to peasants or the children of peasants, under conditions in which nobody thinks he is propounding a religious doctrine to be received or rejected, but only rounding off a story in the most symmetrical way, according to that sort of decorative scheme or pattern that runs through all fairy stories. Others are obviously in their form most emphatically evidence; that is they are testimony that is truth or lies; and it will be very hard for any judge of human nature to think they are lies.

It is admitted that the story of the Stigmata is not a legend but can only be a lie. I mean that it is certainly not a late legendary accretion added afterwards to the fame of St. Francis; but is something that started almost immediately with his earliest biographers. It is practically necessary to suggest that it was a conspiracy; indeed there has been some disposition to put the fraud upon the unfortunate Elias, whom so many parties have been disposed to treat as a useful universal villain. It has been said, indeed, that these early biographers, St. Bonaventura and Celano and the Three Companions, though they declare that St. Francis received the mystical wounds, do not say that they themselves saw those wounds. I do not think this argument conclusive; because it only arises out of the very nature of the narrative. The Three Companions are not in any case making an affidavit; and therefore none of the admitted parts of their story are in the form of an affidavit. They are writing a chronicle of a comparatively impersonal and very objective description. They do not say, "I saw St. Francis's wounds"; they say, "St. Francis received wounds." But neither do they say, "I saw St. Francis go into the Portiuncula"; they say, "St. Francis went into the Portiuncula." But I still cannot understand why they should be trusted as eye-witnesses about the one fact and not trusted as eye-witnesses about the other. It is all of a piece; it would be a most abrupt and abnormal interruption in their way of telling the story if they suddenly began to curse and to swear, and give their names and addresses, and take their oath that they themselves saw and verified the physical facts in question. It seems to me, therefore, that this particular discussion goes back to the general question I have already mentioned; the question of why these chronicles should be credited at all, if they are credited with abounding in the incredible. But that again will probably be found to revert, in the last resort, to the mere fact that some men cannot believe in miracles because they are materialists. That is logical enough; but they are bound to deny the preternatural as much in the testimony of a modern scientific professor as in that of a mediæval monkish chronicler. And there are plenty of professors for them to contradict by this time.

But whatever may be thought of such supernaturalism in the comparatively material and popular sense of supernatural acts, we shall miss the whole point of St. Francis, especially of St. Francis after Alverno, if we do not realise that he was living a supernatural life. And there is more and more of such supernaturalism in his life as he approaches towards his death. This element of the supernatural did not separate him from the natural; for it was the whole point of his position that it united him more perfectly to the natural. It did not make him dismal or dehumanised; for it was the whole meaning of his message that such mysticism makes a man cheerful and humane. But it was the whole point of his position, and it was the whole meaning of his message, that the power that did it was a supernatural power. If this simple distinction were not apparent from the whole of his life, it would be difficult for any one to miss it in reading the account of his death.

In a sense he may be said to have wandered as a dying man, just as he had wandered as a living one. As it became more and more apparent that his health was failing, he seems to have been carried from place to place like a pageant of sickness or almost like a pageant of mortality. He went to Rieti, to Nursia, perhaps to Naples, certainly to Cortona by the lake of Perugia. But there is something profoundly pathetic, and full of great problems, in the fact that at last, as it would seem, his flame of life leapt up and his heart rejoiced when they saw afar

off on the Assisian hill the solemn pillars of the Portiuncula. He who had become a vagabond for the
sake of a vision, he who had denied himself all sense
of place and possession, he whose whole gospel and
glory it was to be homeless, received like a Parthian
shot from nature, the sting of the sense of home. He
also had his *maladie du clocher*, his sickness of
the spire; though his spire was higher than ours.
"Never," he cried with the sudden energy of strong
spirits in death, "never give up this place. If you
would go anywhere or make any pilgrimage, return
always to your home; for this is the holy house of
God." And the procession passed under the arches
of his home; and he lay down on his bed and his
brethren gathered round him for the last long vigil.
It seems to me no moment for entering into the subsequent disputes about which successors he blessed
or in what form and with what significance. In that
one mighty moment he blessed us all.

After he had taken farewell of some of his nearest
and especially some of his oldest friends, he was
lifted at his own request off his own rude bed and
laid on the bare ground; as some say clad only in a
hair-shirt, as he had first gone forth into the wintry
woods from the presence of his father. It was the
final assertion of his great fixed idea; of praise and
thanks springing to their most towering height out
of nakedness and nothing. As he lay there we may
be certain that his seared and blinded eyes saw
nothing but their object and their origin. We may be
sure that the soul, in its last inconceivable isolation,
was face to face with nothing less than God Incar-
nate and Christ Crucified. But for the men standing
around him there must have been other thoughts

mingling with these; and many memories must have gathered like ghosts in the twilight, as that day wore on and that great darkness descended in which we all lost a friend.

For what lay dying there was not Dominic of the Dogs of God, a leader in logical and controversial wars that could be reduced to a plan and handed on like a plan; a master of a machine of democratic discipline by which others could organise themselves. What was passing from the world was a person; a poet; an outlook on life like a light that was never after on sea or land; a thing not to be replaced or repeated while the earth endures. It has been said that there was only one Christian, who died on the cross; it is truer to say in this sense that there was only one Franciscan, whose name was Francis. Huge and happy as was the popular work he left behind him, there was something that he could not leave behind, any more than a landscape painter can leave his eyes in his will. It was an artist in life who was here called to be an artist in death; and he had a better right than Nero, his anti-type, to say *Qualis artifex pereo.* For Nero's life was full of posing for the occasion like that of an actor; while the Umbrian's had a natural and continuous grace like that of an athlete. But St. Francis had better things to say and better things to think about, and his thoughts were caught upwards where we cannot follow them, in divine and dizzy heights to which death alone can lift us up.

Round about him stood the brethren in their brown habits, those that had loved him even if they afterwards disputed with each other. There was Bernard, his first friend, and Angelo, who had served as his secretary, and Elias, his successor, whom tradition tried to turn into a sort of Judas, but who seems to have been little worse than an official in the wrong place. His tragedy was that he had a Franciscan habit without a Franciscan heart, or at any rate with a very un-Franciscan head. But though he made a bad Franciscan, he might have made a decent Dominican. Anyhow, there is no reason to doubt that he loved Francis, for ruffians and savages did that. Anyhow he stood among the rest as the hours passed and the shadows lengthened in the house of the Portiuncula; and nobody need think so ill of him as to suppose that his thoughts were then in the tumultuous future, in the ambitions and controversies of his later years.

A man might fancy that the birds must have known when it happened; and made some motion in the evening sky. As they had once, according to the tale, scattered to the four winds of heaven in the pattern of a cross at his signal of dispersion, they might now have written in such dotted lines a more awful augury across the sky. Hidden in the woods perhaps were little cowering creatures never again to be so much noticed and understood; and it has been said that animals are sometimes conscious of things to which man, their spiritual superior, is for the moment blind. We do not know whether any shiver passed through all the thieves and the outcasts and the outlaws, to tell them what had happened to him who never knew the nature of scorn.

But at least in the passages and porches of the Portiuncula there was a sudden stillness, where all the brown figures stood like bronze statues; for the stopping of the great heart that had not broken till it held the world.

CHAPTER X

The Testament of St. Francis

In one sense doubtless it is a sad irony that St. Francis, who all his life had desired all men to agree, should have died amid increasing disagreements. But we must not exaggerate this discord, as some have done, so as to turn it into a mere defeat of all his ideals. There are some who represent his work as having been merely ruined by the wickedness of the world, or what they always assume to be the even greater wickedness of the Church.

This little book is an essay on St. Francis and not on the Franciscan Order, still less on the Catholic Church or the Papacy or the policy pursued towards the extreme Franciscans or the Fraticelli. It is therefore only necessary to note in a very few words what was the general nature of the controversy that raged after the great saint's death, and to some extent troubled the last days of his life. The dominant detail was the interpretation of the vow of poverty, or the refusal of all possessions. Nobody so far as I know ever proposed to interfere with the vow of the individual friar that he would have no individual possessions. Nobody, that is, proposed to interfere with his negation of private property. But some Franciscans, invoking the authority of Francis on their side, went further than this and further I think than anybody else has ever gone. They proposed to abolish not only private property but property. That is, they refused to be corporately responsible for anything at all; for any buildings or stores or tools; they refused to own them collectively even when they used them collectively. It is perfectly true that many, especially among the first supporters of this view, were men of a splendid and selfless spirit, wholly devoted to the great saint's ideal. It is also perfectly true that the Pope and the authorities of the Church did not think this conception was a workable arrangement, and went so far in modifying it as to set aside certain clauses in the great saint's will. But it is not at all easy to see that it *was* a workable arrangement or even an arrangement at all; for it was really a refusal to arrange anything. Everybody knew of course that Franciscans were communists; but this was not so much being a communist as being an anarchist. Surely upon any argument somebody or something must be answerable for what happened to or in or concerning a number of historic edifices and ordinary goods and chattels. Many idealists of a socialistic sort, notably of the school of Mr. Shaw or Mr. Wells, have treated this dispute as if it were merely a case of the tyranny of wealthy and wicked pontiffs crushing the true Christianity of Christian Socialists. But in truth this extreme ideal was in a sense the very reverse of Socialist, or even social. Precisely the thing which these enthusiasts refused was that social ownership

on which Socialism is built; what they primarily refused to do was what Socialists primarily exist to do;
to own legally in their corporate capacity. Nor is it
true that the tone of the Popes towards the enthusiasts was merely harsh and hostile. The Pope maintained for a long time a compromise which he had
specially designed to meet their own conscientious
objections; a compromise by which the Papacy itself
held the property in a kind of trust for the owners
who refused to touch it. The truth is that this incident shows two things which are common enough
in Catholic history, but very little understood by the
journalistic history of industrial civilisation. It shows
that the Saints were sometimes great men when the
Popes were small men. But it also shows that great
men are sometimes wrong when small men are right.
And it will be found, after all, very difficult for any
candid and clear-headed outsider to deny that the
Pope was right, when he insisted that the world was
not made only for Franciscans.

For that was what was behind the quarrel. At the
back of this particular practical question there was
something much larger and more momentous, the
stir and wind of which we can feel as we read the
controversy. We might go so far as to put the ultimate truth thus. St. Francis was so great and original
a man that he had something in him of what makes
the founder of a religion. Many of his followers were
more or less ready, in their hearts, to treat him as the
founder of a religion. They were willing to let the
Franciscan spirit escape from Christendom as the
Christian spirit had escaped from Israel. They were
willing to let it eclipse Christendom as the Christian
spirit had eclipsed Israel. Francis, the fire that ran

through the roads of Italy, was to be the beginning of a conflagration in which the old Christian civilisation was to be consumed. That was the point the Pope had to settle; whether Christendom should absorb Francis or Francis Christendom. And he decided rightly, apart from the duties of his place; for the Church could include all that was good in the Franciscans and the Franciscans could not include all that was good in the Church.

There is one consideration which, though sufficiently clear in the whole story, has not perhaps been sufficiently noted, especially by those who cannot see the case for a certain Catholic common sense larger even than Franciscan enthusiasm. Yet it arises out of the very merits of the man whom they so rightly admire. Francis of Assisi, as has been said again and again, was a poet; that is, he was a person who could express his personality. Now it is everywhere the mark of this sort of man that his very limitations make him larger. He is what he is, not only by what he has, but in some degree by what he has not. But the limits that make the lines of such a personal portrait cannot be made the limits of all humanity. St. Francis is a very strong example of this quality in the man of genius, that in him even what is negative is positive, because it is part of a character. An excellent example of what I mean may be found in his attitude towards learning and scholarship. He ignored and in some degree discouraged books and book-learning; and from his own point of view and that of his own work in the world he was absolutely right. The whole point of his message was to be so simple that the village idiot could understand it. The whole point of his point of view was that it looked out freshly upon a fresh world, that might have been made that morning. Save for the great primal things, the Creation and the Story of Eden, the first Christmas and the first Easter, the world had no history. But is it desired or desirable that the whole Catholic Church should have no history?

It is perhaps the chief suggestion of this book that St. Francis walked the world like the Pardon of God. I mean that his appearance marked the moment when men could be reconciled not only to God but to nature and, most difficult of all, to themselves. For it marked the moment when all the stale paganism that had poisoned the ancient world was at last worked out of the social system. He opened the gates of the Dark Ages as of a prison of purgatory, where men had cleansed themselves as hermits in the desert or heroes in the barbarian wars. It was in fact his whole function to tell men to start afresh and, in that sense, to tell them to forget. If they were to turn over a new leaf and begin a fresh page with the first large letters of the alphabet, simply drawn and brilliantly coloured in the early mediæval manner, it was clearly a part of that particular childlike cheerfulness that they should paste down the old page that was all black and bloody with horrid things. For instance, I have already noted that there is not a trace in the poetry of this first Italian poet of all that pagan mythology which lingered long after paganism. The first Italian poet seems the only man in the world who has never even heard of Virgil. This was exactly right for the special sense in which he is the first Italian poet. It is quite right that he should call a nightingale a nightingale, and

not have its song spoilt or saddened by the terrible
tales of Itylus or Procne. In short, it is really quite
right and quite desirable that St. Francis should
never have heard of Virgil. But do we really desire
that Dante should never have heard of Virgil? Do
we really desire that Dante should never have read
any pagan mythology? It has been truly said that
the use that Dante makes of such fables is altogether
part of a deeper orthodoxy; that his huge heathen
fragments, his gigantic figures of Minos or of Charon,
only give a hint of some enormous natural religion
behind all history and from the first foreshadowing
the Faith. It is well to have the Sybil as well as Da-
vid in the Dies Iræ. That St. Francis would have
burned all the leaves of all the books of the Sybil,
in exchange for one fresh leaf from the nearest tree,
is perfectly true; and perfectly proper to St. Francis. But it is good to have the Dies Iræ as well as the
Canticle of the Sun.

By this thesis, in short, the coming of St. Francis
was like the birth of a child in a dark house, lifting
its doom; a child that grows up unconscious of the
tragedy and triumphs over it by his innocence. In
him it is necessarily not only innocence but ignorance. It is the essence of the story that *he* should
pluck at the green grass without knowing it grows
over a murdered man or climb the apple-tree without knowing it was the gibbet of a suicide. It was
such an amnesty and reconciliation that the freshness of the Franciscan spirit brought to all the
world. But it does not follow that it ought to impose
its ignorance on all the world. And I think it would
have tried to impose it on all the world. For some
Franciscans it would have seemed right that Fran-

ciscan poetry should expel Benedictine prose. For
the symbolic child it was quite rational. It was right
enough that for such a child the world should be a
large new nursery with blank white-washed walls,
on which he could draw his own pictures in chalk
in the childish fashion, crude in outline and gay in
colour; the beginnings of all our art. It was right
enough that to him such a nursery should seem the
most magnificent mansion of the imagination of
man. But in the Church of God are many mansions.

Every heresy has been an effort to narrow the
Church. If the Franciscan movement had turned
into a new religion, it would after all have been a
narrow religion. In so far as it did turn here and
there into a heresy, it was a narrow heresy. It did
what heresy always does; it set the mood against the
mind. The mood was indeed orginally the good and
glorious mood of the great St. Francis, but it was not
the whole mind of God or even of man. And it is a
fact that the mood itself degenerated, as the mood
turned into a monomania. A sect that came to be
called the Fraticelli declared themselves the true
sons of St. Francis and broke away from the compromises of Rome in favour of what they would have
called the complete programme of Assisi. In a very
little while these loose Franciscans began to look as
ferocious as Flagellants. They launched new and
violent vetoes; they denounced marriage; that is,
they denounced mankind. In the name of the most
human of saints they declared war upon humanity.
They did not perish particularly through being per-
secuted; many of them were eventually persuaded;
and the unpersuadable rump of them that remained
remained without producing anything in the least

calculated to remind anybody of the real St. Francis. What was the matter with these people was that they were mystics; mystics and nothing else but mystics; mystics and not Catholics; mystics and not Christians; mystics and not men. They rotted away because, in the most exact sense, they would not listen to reason. And St. Francis, however wild and romantic his gyrations might appear to many, always hung on to reason by one invisible and indestructible hair.

The great saint was sane; and with the very sound of the word sanity, as at a deeper chord struck upon a harp, we come back to something that was indeed deeper than everything about him that seemed an almost elvish eccentricity. He was not a mere eccentric because he was always turning towards the centre and heart of the maze; he took the queerest and most zigzag short cuts through the wood, but he was always going home. He was not only far too humble to be an heresiarch, but he was far too human to desire to be an extremist, in the sense of an exile at the ends of the earth. The sense of humour which salts all the stories of his escapades alone prevented him from ever hardening into the solemnity of sectarian self-righteousness. He was by nature ready to admit that he was wrong; and if his followers had on some practical points to admit that he was wrong, they only admitted that he was wrong in order to prove that he was right. For it is they, his real followers, who have really proved that he was right and even in transcending some of his negations have triumphantly extended and interpreted his truth. The Franciscan order did not fossilise or break off short like something of which the true purpose has been frustrated by official tyranny or internal treason. It was this, the central and orthodox trunk of it, that afterwards bore fruit for the world. It counted among its sons Bonaventura, the great mystic, and Bernardino, the popular preacher, who filled Italy with the very beatific buffooneries of a Jongleur de Dieu. It counted Raymond Lully with his strange learning and his large and daring plans for the conversion of the world; a man intensely individual exactly as St. Francis was intensely individual. It counted Roger Bacon, the first naturalist whose experiments with light and water had all the luminous quaintness that belongs to the beginnings of natural history; and whom even the most material scientists have hailed as a father of science. It is not merely true that these were great men who did great work for the world; it is also true that they were a certain kind of men keeping the spirit and savour of a certain kind of man, that we can recognise in them a taste and tang of audacity and simplicity, and know them for the sons of St. Francis.

For that is the full and final spirit in which we should turn to St. Francis; in the spirit of thanks for what he has done. He was above all things a great giver; and he cared chiefly for the best kind of giving which is called thanksgiving. If another great man wrote a grammar of assent, he may well be said to have written a grammar of acceptance; a grammar of gratitude. He understood down to its very depths the theory of thanks; and its depths are a bottomless abyss. He knew that the praise of God stands on its strongest ground when it stands on nothing. He knew that we can best measure the towering miracle of the mere fact of existence if we realise that but for some strange mercy we should not even exist. And something of that larger truth is repeated in a lesser form in our own relations with so mighty a maker of history. He also is a giver of things we could not have even thought of for ourselves; he also is too great for anything but gratitude. From him came a whole awakening of the world and a dawn in which all shapes and colours could be seen anew. The mighty men of genius who made the Christian civilisation that we know appear in history almost as his servants and imitators. Before Dante was, he had given poetry to Italy; before St. Louis ruled, he had risen as the tribune of the poor; and before Giotto had painted the pictures, he had enacted the scenes. That great painter who began the whole human inspiration of European painting had himself gone to St. Francis to be inspired. It is said that when St. Francis staged in his own simple fashion a Nativity Play of Bethlehem, with kings and angels in the stiff and gay mediæval garments and the golden wigs that stood for haloes, a miracle was wrought full of the Franciscan glory. The Holy Child was a wooden doll or bambino, and it was said that he embraced it and that the image came to life in his arms. He assuredly was not thinking of lesser things; but we may at least say that one thing came to life in his arms; and that was the thing that we call the drama. Save for his intense individual love of song, he did not perhaps himself embody this spirit in any of these arts. He was the spirit that was embodied. He was the spiritual essence and substance that walked the world, before any one had seen these things in visible forms derived from it: a wandering fire as if from nowhere, at which men more material could

light both torches and tapers. He was the soul of
mediæval civilisation before it even found a body.
Another and quite different stream of spiritual inspiration derives largely from him; all that reform-
ing energy of mediæval and modern times that goes
to the burden of *Deus est Deus Pauperum*. His abstract ardour for human beings was in a multitude
of just mediæval laws against the pride and cruelty
of riches; it is to-day behind much that is loosely
called Christian Socialist and can more correctly be
called Catholic Democrat. Neither on the artistic
nor the social side would anybody pretend that
these things would not have existed without him;
yet it is strictly true to say that we cannot now imagine them without him; since he has lived and
changed the world.

And something of that sense of impotence which
was more than half his power will descend on any
one who knows what that inspiration has been in
history, and can only record it in a series of strag-
gling and meagre sentences. He will know something of what St. Francis meant by the great and
good debt that cannot be paid. He will feel at once
the desire to have done infinitely more and the fu-
tility of having done anything. He will know what
it is to stand under such a deluge of a dead man's
marvels, and have nothing in return to establish
against it; to have nothing to set up under the over-
hanging, overwhelming arches of such a temple of
time and eternity, but this brief candle burnt out so
quickly before his shrine.